AIMED & READY

NICO SMIT

AIMED & READY

YOUR PULLBACK IS A SETUP FOR YOUR COMEBACK!

Aimed & Ready Copyright © 2026 by Nico Smit

Nico Smit's blog: nicosmitblog.com

All rights reserved. No part of this book may be reproduced in any manner whatsoever without written permission except in the case of brief quotations embodied in critical articles and reviews.
First Printing by Ingram Spark, 2026

A copy of this title, Aimed & Ready, is held at the
National Library of Australia.

ISBN: 978-1-7644559-1-6
eISBN: 978-1-7644559-2-3

Scriptures taken from the New King James Version®. Copyright © 1982 by Thomas Nelson. Used by permission. All rights reserved.
Scripture quotations marked (NLT) are taken from the Holy Bible, New Living Translation, copyright ©1996, 2004, 2015 by Tyndale House Foundation. Used by permission of Tyndale House Publishers, Carol Stream, Illinois 60188. All rights reserved.

Published by Bekker Media on behalf of Yeshua Collective, Pty Ltd,
58 Channel Highway, Kingston TAS 7050.

Cover design by Matthew de Livera, @mdfilmcreative

Edited by Bekker Media, New South Wales, Australia
www.bekker.media

Original picture courtesy of Unsplash by Zoltan Tasi

NOTE FROM THE AUTHOR

I recognize that many of you have turned to this book in a time of desperation, disheartenment, and yearning—a deep hunger for something you realize only God can provide. I understand that you may be believing, hoping, and perhaps even praying that the answers you seek will be revealed within these pages. This is indeed a magnificent reason to delve into this book. However, I must gently remind you that not all the answers you want lie here. This is not the Bible. It is essential to immerse yourself in your Bible, for it is there that God speaks most clearly to your heart. This book aims to guide you, minister to you and illuminate what to seek, but the true wisdom and understanding you desire will come from your personal engagement with Scripture itself. Make sure you spend time in it.

Blessings,
Nico

An Audiobook and a Devotional are available
for Aimed & Ready

CONTENTS

Note from the Author vii
Endorsements xi
Foreword xix

Prologue 1

PART I: THE PULLBACK 5
Introduction 7
Chapter 1: The Start of a New Beginning 15
Chapter 2: There Has to Be a Pullback 27
Chapter 3: Be Still: It's a Holy HUSH 37
Chapter 4: You're in an In-Between Place 49

PART II: THE HAND OF THE ARCHER 59
Chapter 5: Are You Ready for What's Coming? 61
Chapter 6: Jesus Practiced Pullback Often 69
Chapter 7: Surrendered to the Archer 79
Chapter 8: Don't Wind Up if You're Not Willing to Let Go 87

PART III: PRAYER, AIM, RESET, FIRE 95
Chapter 9: Prayers That Breakthrough 97
Chapter 10: A Reset is a Re-Aim with Purpose 107
Chapter 11: Stay Aimed: Locked on Target
              Until You're Fired 117
Chapter 12: Breakthrough Happens
              When the Arrow Hits the Mark 125

PART IV: THE COMEBACK STORY 133
Chapter 13: Ziklag: Pullback Before Promotion 135
Chapter 14: The Launch: Rockets, Rowers,
         Warriors, Arrows 145

PART V: THE MARK OF HOPE 153
Chapter 15: Hope: The Ultimate Comeback 155

Conclusion: Aimed & Ready 163
About the Author 168

ENDORSEMENTS

I met Nico Smit in 2018 and was immediately struck by his apostolic grace, prophetic insight, and genuine pastoral warmth. Over the years, I've watched him faithfully navigate various seasons with determination, humility, and a clear sense of God-given purpose.

Aimed & Ready is a timely and deeply encouraging prophetic manual for anyone who feels their life has been pulled back rather than pushed forward. As I read, I was reminded of seasons in my own journey where transition brought confusion, tension, silence, and ultimately surrender—only to discover those moments were preparation for God's appointed time of promotion, blessing, and fulfilled purpose.

The prophetic often hears and sees what others cannot yet perceive. Nico brings prophetic clarity, wisdom, biblical and theological depth, reminding us that God never wastes seasons of tension, silence or motion. As he so powerfully states, "What feels like pressure is often alignment," - "what feels like delay is preparation for impact." - "God does not waste motion. Every adjustment serves purpose. Every correction builds capacity."

Page after page is filled with insight—more than once I found myself saying out loud, "Wow!" Circling back to ponder what I had just read!

This book will encourage both leaders and believers to trust God and His timing, remain aligned, and move forward with renewed faith and confidence through surrender to His greater purpose. As Nico writes, "Surrender your entire being into the hands of Someone who knows you better than you know yourself." Breakthrough comes to those willing to wait, submit to the process, and refuse to rely on their own strength. What feels like a pullback is often God "stabilizing our spirit" for the breakthrough ahead.

Every chapter stirred my spirit to allow God to do a deeper work in me for His purpose and glory. I stopped and read portions to my wife with excitement!

I believe *Aimed & Ready* will bless many who are patiently waiting and faithfully stewarding seasons of silence and preparation. Read it slowly. Let the words penetrate your heart, energize your prayer life, and shape your daily walk. This book will saturate you with faith and hope, align your heart to correction, and strengthen your confidence in God's purpose.

Thank you, Nico for a prophetic masterpiece!

Gary Heyes, Ontario, Canada
Prophet and Pastor
Founder, Speak Life Global

* * *

I wholeheartedly endorse this powerful and timely book by Pastor Nico Smit. Having walked in full-time ministry since 1999, I have learned to recognize when a prophetic voice carries genuine weight, clarity, and anointing—and Nico's voice is unmistakably one of them.

Nico has been more than a colleague in ministry to me; he has been a brother, a fellow worker in the Kingdom of God, and a trusted friend over many years. His prophetic ministry is marked by depth, humility, and accuracy, and his words consistently carry both conviction and hope. This book is no exception. In fact, it contains words I deeply needed to read in this season of my own journey.

This is not a book written merely to inspire—it is written to realign. The prophetic insight it offers to current leaders and emerging leaders alike is both vital and necessary for spiritual maturity. It speaks clearly into seasons of pressure, delay, and uncertainty, reminding us that God is never absent in the pullback, but intentionally preparing us for His purposes.

One line in particular has stayed with me: "Delay is not lost time. It is invested time." That truth alone has adjusted much of my thinking and reignited my confidence in God's timing and direction for my life—and I believe it will do the same for many others.

This book is truly life-changing. It reassures us that even in moments of intense pressure, God is positioning us to move forward. I am deeply grateful to Pastor Nico for releasing this prophetic word at such a crucial time. "Our current pullback is not our end—it is preparation for a powerful comeback."

Ryan Laubscher, Cape Town, South Africa
Pastor, Evangelist and Community Leader
Lead Pastor Overflow Church, Fish Hoek
Head of Evangelism in the Western Cape,
Full Gospel Church of God, South Africa,
Chairman at Kingdom Encounter SA NPO, Cape Town, South Africa

* * *

I thoroughly enjoyed reading Ps Nico's latest book, *Aimed & Ready*.

Nico reaches deep into your soul and spirit and infuses great hope in seasons of uncertainty and delay.

It re-anchors you to Jesus Christ, to His hope, His plan, and His future for your life when everything feels uncertain.

This book brings renewed purpose, fresh resolve, and the strength to keep standing in barren seasons. Seasons where there is no fruit on the tree, where transitions feel awkward, and where the silence of waiting on God's promises feels uncomfortable and long.

Ps Nico writes with conviction and depth, reminding us that delay does not mean denial and silence does not mean absence. *Aimed & Ready* calls you back to faith, hope, endurance, and unwavering trust in Jesus.

I would highly recommend Nico's book to anyone. This is a must-read.

Chelsea Hagen, Sunshine Coast, Australia
Pastor, Leader and Prophetic Minister
Hagen Ministries, Nashville USA
Founder, Fire Church Ministries, Australia

* * *

I was honored when Nico asked me to endorse his new book, but I didn't realize what a powerful book it was until I read the manuscript. Every single chapter is packed with prophetic insight and revelation. As I began to read, God ministered to my own heart in a profound way. This book teaches us to not let adversity discourage us, but to press into the call of God with renewed determination. It takes a true warrior to endure under pressure - and that's exactly what we are created for.

This book will challenge the reader to arise in boldness, shatter limitations, and be ready to step into God's calling on their lives. Your trials will not only transform you but birth an amazing testimony for God's glory. The assignments from the enemy are meant to divert your attention from the Lord and your purpose, but as you pursue your vision and the dream that Jesus has placed in your heart, your perseverance will propel you into your destiny.

The Lord is about to release a second wind to those in the body of Christ who are spiritually lethargic and have lost their zeal. They once had a passion for the Word of God and the gifts of the Holy Spirit, but they got worn down by the relentless pressures of life. If this is you, this book will encourage you to rise again and become the person who God intended you to be. You will discover that God has so much more for you.

Elaine Tavolacci, New York NY, USA
Prophetic Minister, Author and Publisher
Publisher of "A Word in Season", "The Voice Of Breakthrough" and "The Voice Of Prophecy"
Elaine Tavolacci Ministries, www.ElaineTavolacci.com

* * *

It was a joy to read my friend Nico Smit's latest book, *Aimed & Ready*!

In the book, Nico shares numerous prophetic insights and powerful word pictures regarding the spiritual health of everyday Christians in our post Covid age. Instead of despairing our apparent setbacks, Nico exhorts us to look deeper into the places God has set us. He coaches us out of disillusionment, desperation and discontent to see that God is instead positioning us. What feels like a setback is actually God pulling us back, steadying us, aligning us, and then launching us toward His target for our lives.

For me, Nico's insights regarding control are invaluable and timely. I also appreciate what he wrote about the life of King David at Ziklag.

Finally, he caps it all off with a powerful prayer for our patience and understanding of God's process of preparing us to fly right into the bullseye of His plan for our lives. The entire book is like a decoder ring for where you may be finding yourself currently positioned; I cannot recommend it highly enough.

Mel(vain) Donyes, Hudson WI, USA
Pastor and Missionary,
Chairman at South African Evangelistic Mission Board (USA)

* * *

I first met Ps Nico Smit six years ago at a conference in Brisbane, Australia. I had the honor of hosting him in the speaker's room where I just watched and observed him. I heard him minister for the first time after that and I still remember saying to myself, 'I want to know God like he does.' I can assure you the man you meet in these pages is exactly who he appears to be. Nico isn't someone who looks for a platform. His laid down life is a platform for the Lord to stand on. He is someone who has learned to sit with the Lord, listen and speak from that place of deep intimacy. You feel it the moment you begin reading this book.

I believe *Aimed & Ready* will be a manual for the soul born out of walking with God through seasons that don't always make sense. Nico carries a genuine heart for revival. What struck me most was how steadying this book feels. In a culture of constant noise and pressure, Nico offers clarity and a reason to trust God's timing. Something that stood out to me was this statement, 'Don't mistake the pullback for punishment'. A pullback is a setup for a comeback. If you're in a season of waiting, stretching, or hiding, this book will be a lifeline to you. I truly believe it will help you rest, realign, and trust the Lord's heart all over again.

Joshua Sawiris, Nashville TN, USA
Pastor and Revivalist
Senior Pastor, Glory City Church Nashville

* * *

Battles are never won by giving up, but by getting up over and over again. That is the journey of life when we live for God. Prophet Nico Smit is one of those people - a warrior, a never-give-up person with a steadfast, immovable spirit that has come through the fires of affliction and adversity. What a great title to his book – *Aimed & Ready*!

Aimed and ready for whatever life unfolds, the good and the not so good, the victories and the losses are all part of the journey of life in becoming an overcomer and to being a conqueror. I personally recommend Prophet Nico's book. It has keys and principals that will prepare you and inspire you to keep running the race of faith regardless of the challenges that life brings.

Prophet Nico has had many challenges, and he has a proven record of overcoming them and is a testimony of God's amazing grace and the power of the Holy Spirit that has empowered him and enabled him to be a conqueror. His love for the people of God to become overcomers and to be conquerors continues to champion us all. You will not be disappointed as you read *Aimed & Ready*. You will gain eternal knowledge, understanding and strategies to overcome in the difficult seasons and continue to walk the journey of life as a conqueror.

Congratulations Prophet Nico, on producing another book to Champion His Church in Australia and the Nations.

Ada Boland, Toowoomba QLD, Australia
Prophet and Pastor
Indigenous Apostolic Prophetic Voice
Founder Prophetic Voices of the Land

FOREWORD

We feel it in our bones. There's a shift in the atmosphere, an expectant excitement. We know something is coming. We have caught glimpses of it – quiet awakenings, prodigals returning, a hunger for more of the knowledge and presence of God.

In *Aimed & Ready*, Nico Smit articulates beautifully what we are all feeling - the stretch, the discomfort, the waiting, the not-knowing and the shaking. He doesn't just describe the spiritual atmosphere in this season, he gives us the reason why we feel the way we do and insight into what we can do about it.

Nico has learnt well from Jesus. He brilliantly uses allegory to reveal the truth about what to expect when God pours His Spirit out on all flesh. His metaphor of an archer pulling back the arrow – aiming it, steadying it and launching it – powerfully and prophetically illustrates what God is doing across the earth. As Nico describes the action of the Archer and His arrows, you understand the tension that many are feeling in this season. You feel an inexorable drawing to come aside, to be quiet, to ponder, to inquire of the Lord. You want to slow down because you realize there is no other way to speed up, except to surrender to the hand of the Creator who crafted you as His arrow – with a target in mind (Ephesians. 2:10).

You are not destined to remain in the dark, hidden and mystified by what's going on around you. You are not destined to stay silent, scared to speak up. You are not destined to live feeling numb and confused. You are destined to live in the light, knowing exactly what God is doing, what you were created for, to speak up with courage, conviction and passion. You were born for such a time as this.

Nico reminds us that as we yield during the stretching times, God refines our focus and we see the target more clearly. At times, as we feel His nearness, we discover that we may not be looking at the same target the Archer is aiming us at. As we are led by His Spirit, we re-focus and allow Him to change our trajectory, even though it can be uncomfortable and counterintuitive.

So, if you are feeling tired, worn out by all the bad news and constant pressure, confused by current affairs, or feeling like it's taking forever for God to move, take heart! God has given us prophetic voices like Nico Smit to lift our heads and change our perspective. In the pages of this book, you will find hope. Faith will rise in you, and you will once again have a reason to trust your Creator that there is a purpose to life and, more specifically, a purpose to *your* life.

Nico is a true prophetic voice. He refocuses us on what *God* is doing in the earth, so that we can move in step with His Spirit. We need God's guidance to help us see what is going on in the unseen realm of the spirit so that we don't depend only on what we see in the physical realm. Truly, there is more hope, life and beauty in the world than we could ever imagine. As the author of the book of Hebrews says, "the word of God is alive and active" (Hebrews 4:12). God does not sit idly by, impassively observing His creation. No! He is in us and on us, alive and active, fulfilling His promises and finishing what He began in Jesus Christ. God is preparing us for the great harvest which is to come. So, if you feel like giving up, or feel that you have failed, that you heard wrong … wait just a little longer. I join my voice with Nico's and say, "Hold on! You're not alone. God is about to launch His 'arrows'."

But forget all that — it is nothing compared to what I am going to do. For I am about to do something new. See, I have already begun! Do you not see it? - Isaiah 43:18-19

It is not by force nor by strength, but by my Spirit, says the Lord of Heaven's Armies. -Zechariah 4:6

In Nico's words, "The size of the coming harvest demands a launch greater than human strategy. It will require supernatural timing, supernatural unity, supernatural boldness, and supernatural empowerment by the Spirit". So, God is preparing us now for what lies ahead.

Thank you, Nico. Your words are like arrows hitting their targets.

Stacey Campbell, Santa Maria CA, USA
Prophet, Author and International Speaker
Founder of Shiloh Global
Founder of the International Prophetic Council
Facilitator of the Canadian Prophetic Council
Honorary member of the International Apostolic Council of Prophetic Elders

PROLOGUE

As you open this book, you may be someone who has listened to prophetic words and encouragement for years, yet lately you find yourself wondering, *God, where are You?*
You've heard *forward*, but all you've felt is backward.
You've heard *promotion*, but all you can see is pain.
You've heard *restoration*, but your life doesn't feel whole yet.
You expected *elevation*, but your experience has looked like stretching and humbling.

Even while holding onto faith, your heart still cries out: *God, where are You? Where are Your promises? Will any of them become real for me? I need to know.*

IT IS FOR YOU THAT I WROTE THIS BOOK.

What if your PULLBACK is needed so that your COMEBACK can be God's PUSH FORWARD for your life? I believe many who read these pages will recognize the difficulties, disappointments, and tensions of a time when everything felt off-track. You may not have found words for it, but you've sensed it. A pull. A pressure. A retreat. A winding back. Some have felt loss, frustration, heaviness that didn't feel holy, and silence that felt like abandonment. You haven't felt blessed.

Before you decide that season was defeat, pause for a moment.

Lift your eyes.

Notice where God is pointing you.

Not where circumstances have restricted you.

Notice what He is aligning, not what has been taken. Consider that what you interpreted as breaking may actually have been shaping, and what felt like retreat may have been God positioning you for more. Heaven may have been faithful in ways your emotions never told you and more intentional than your circumstances revealed.

What if you've been placed in a divine wind-up? What if everything you've endured - the setbacks, the confusion, the delays, the prayers that seemed unanswered, hasn't been the evidence of God's distance, but the proof of His preparation? What if He was never distant but deeply involved? What if you are closer to launching into your purpose than you've ever been? What if the chapter you feared was the end of you was actually the beginning of something beautiful heaven has arranged just for you? What if God is aiming you, aligning you, focusing you, preparing you, and making you ready to hit the mark of His best for you?

You are not retreating.
You are not shrinking.
You are not being disqualified or forgotten.
You are being aimed and made ready.

This truth became clear to me as I prepared a message for the Australian Prophetic Summit in September 2025. While waiting on the Lord, I saw a vision: a bow fully drawn, with an arrow held under pressure. At first it looked painful, strained, uncomfortable, and intense. Then I heard the Lord whisper, "It's not what it looks like. What appears to be tension is actually alignment. What feels like discomfort is actually empowerment. The pressure is not evidence that something is wrong, it is proof that something is being aimed. It is evidence that this arrow has a destiny."

A bow cannot launch an arrow without tension. And an arrow cannot soar unless it is first drawn back. Arrows are not made to fall—they are made to soar. Arrows are not made to miss the target - they are made to hit it. The further the pullback, the greater the distance it can go. The greater the pressure, the greater the power. The pain is in the pullback, but the release will be effortless and successful.

Sometimes God's pullback is the very thing that moves us forward. It shifts our trajectory, sharpens our focus, and realigns us with destiny. It protects us from settling for less than His best and reminds us that His purpose reaches further than our plans. The story God has written for your life does not end with you stuck, defeated, or delayed. If that is where you currently are, the story is still unfolding. Your story will be the one He intended from the beginning, filled with purpose, testimony, and resurrection power.

God does not waste His arrows. He does not release them to fall short. His desire is for each one to reach the goal and receive the prize. He is positioning you. Even when it feels as if you're going backward, know that you are gaining momentum by His hand. You are being calibrated for accuracy, impact, and influence.

Let me remind you: seeds must be buried before they break open into life. Burial does not signal the end of destiny; it often signals the beginning of fulfillment. So, don't misread your burial season as expiration. Don't confuse silence with abandonment. And don't mistake the pullback for punishment. A pullback is a setup for a comeback. The greatest victory in history first looked like overwhelming defeat. When Jesus was crucified and buried, hell celebrated, the disciples mourned, and many believed the story was over. What appeared to be loss was actually alignment. What felt like setback became the launching point for resurrection power. The same Jesus who was buried rose with authority, holding the keys of death, hell, and the grave.

This book is a trumpet call to turn your heart, your ears, and your eyes toward heaven. God is inviting His people into something significant.

These pages are not merely a collection of thoughts, inspiration, prophetic reflections, or theology. They are a divine invitation to deeper trust in God's incredible purposes, unlocked through faith. They offer insight into what God is doing in this moment of human story. They carry encouragement for those struggling to interpret their present season and hope for those burdened by waiting, delay, or loss. Within these chapters is vision, hope, power, and a future worth pursuing.

So, wherever you find yourself - exhausted or expectant, wounded or rising, uncertain or full of anticipation, hear this: God has something for you. You are being held between His fingers for the future He designed for you before time began. You are AIMED and READY. Don't let go of trust. Don't allow discouragement to obscure destiny. Take a deep breath. Be still. Rest in His goodness and His timing. Trust His faithfulness. His promises are not fragile, they are "yes and amen" in Jesus Christ.

God is preparing to launch you further than you imagined, into plans bigger than your dreams ever dared to touch. He is setting your influence beyond what you ever envisioned into a radiant future and bursting with His glory.

So now the question becomes sacred:
Will you let God aim you where He wants you?
Will you let Him release you toward the bullseye of His purpose?

If your answer is *yes,* then your comeback has already begun, and your success is already in sight.

PART I: THE PULLBACK

INTRODUCTION

"Fear not, for I am with you; Be not dismayed, for I am your God. I will strengthen you, Yes, I will help you, I will uphold you with My righteous right hand."
— Isaiah 41:10

Many look at their current season and see decline, loss or delay. Heaven sees positioning. We often stand in the middle of quiet ground, empty calendars, closed doors, unanswered questions, and whisper, "Everything went wrong." Yet that very stillness can hide the hand of God - arranging, shifting, preparing, aligning every piece for the word He already spoke over your life.

Never confuse your promotion with your death.

Jesus hung on a cross while hell celebrated. To every natural eye it looked finished. Heaven called it a setup. In that crucified moment Jesus held resurrection power and the keys of death, hell and the grave. The seed went into the ground so a harvest could rise. Burial preceded breakthrough. This pattern did not end at the tomb. God still works this way. A pullback comes before a comeback.

Think of a fruit tree at the end of winter. Branches stand bare, cold, lifeless. Then one day, those same branches explode with blossoms, full and bright. One moment empty, the next heavy with color and promise. Fields of tilled soil hide thousands of seeds. No one sees movement under that layer of earth yet roots push down and life pushes up. To the seed, burial felt like the end; in God's design it marked the beginning of increase.

So, if you say, "That sounds bold, risky, even unrealistic," go ask the orchard in spring. Ask the field under a rising sun. Creation knows this rhythm well. Pullback, then life. Pressure, then growth. Silence, then sound. Apparent backward motion, then unstoppable forward surge.

Picture an ancient catapult on a battlefield. Warriors did not wind it back for decoration. Soldiers did not strain at the ropes for entertainment. It took strength, timing, unity, effort, then stillness while the arm locked in high tension. In that tight, stretched pause every soldier knows: something heavy is about to fly. Everything in that moment says, "We are ready, we are loaded, we are aimed."

Right now, many churches across the earth stand in that kind of moment. Leaders look at numbers, culture, politics, confusion, pressure on every side and feel as if they have been pushed onto the back foot. Heaven says, "No retreat. Windup." This is a Ziklag hour for the body of Christ - a moment where loss and fire have visited the camp, yet God speaks, "Pursue, for you shall surely overtake and recover all."

In this season the Spirit of God keeps highlighting one word in my heart: MOVEMENT. Not random activity, but Spirit-breathed movement. I see a people who have been still in the right way—aligned, listening, letting God aim them—now stepping out with fresh boldness. I see churches lighting up again with hunger, worship, holiness, compassion and supernatural faith. I see a rising momentum of miracles and mercy. I carry an unshakable conviction that God is doing something fresh and powerful on the earth to TURN HEARTS BACK TO HIM.

To move with Him we need our aim back. The reason many sink in the middle of their own story is the same reason Peter began to sink on the water: he moved his attention off Jesus and onto the wind and waves. When eyes lock on storms, fear rules. When eyes lock on the One walking on top of the storm, faith rises. God is calling His people: "Lift your gaze. Fix your eyes again on My Son. Aim your life at My glory, not at the enemy."

"Behold, I am doing a new thing!
Now it springs up; do you not perceive it?"
— Isaiah 43:19

God had more to show me about the vision I saw of the bow and arrow:

"It is not what it looks like. You see a bow that hurts and an arrow under pressure. I see preparation. Do not focus on the strain, the cost, the strength it took to pull the arrow back. This is a beginning, not an ending. Watch where I point you. I am using this moment to aim you, to set your course, to line you up with what I made ready long before you saw it.

The pullback is why you will go far. The more fully you allow Me to prime you, the larger the outcome will be. You cannot see every detail yet, but you will. When you fly, you will see your advantage, you will see your assignment with clarity. The pain sits in the pullback. The release carries no pain. It took much to pull you this far; it will not take much to send you across the sky into your target. Your speed, your reach, your accuracy will flow out of your willingness to trust Me in the pullback."

Many already sense this in their spirit. They feel the weight of a prophetic pause. They look up, not down. They see the bow bent, the string tight, the arrow held. They feel Heaven's breath gathering. They have chosen surrender, instead of resistance. They have allowed their Archer to aim them, even when that aim cuts across personal comfort, plans and timelines. They stand ready for firing into assignments prepared in advance.

These pages carry a heart's cry: to make sense of that pressure. To show what God has done, what He is doing right now, and what He is aligning you to step into. If you feel as if life pulled you backward; if you carry scars, disappointments, delays, losses and questions; if your soul says, "I thought we were going forward, why does everything feel like retreat?"—then lean in. Look again at where His hand is pointing. Notice the target in His eyes. Consider how powerful your life will become after this divine windup. You stand on the edge of the greatest comeback you have seen in your lifetime.

Part of the spark for this whole comeback message came while preparing for a gathering. I shared a story told by an American football coach. He said something like this:

"There is a guy - you knock him down, he stays down. I do not want him. Then there is a player - you knock him down, he gets up. You knock him down again, he stays down. I do not want him either. Then there is a man - you knock him down, he gets up. You knock him down, he gets up again. You knock him down a third time, again he rises. I do not want him either. I want you to find the man who knocks everybody else down—bring me that man. That's the man I am looking for."

YOU ARE THE ONE THE LORD WANTS! Not because you've been knocked down a few times, but because God sees you as the one who can be aimed and useful! Heaven is not impressed with how many times you have fallen. Heaven calls out the one who finally realizes, "In Christ, I am not the one always lying on the ground. I am called, anointed and sent to bring giants down. I get up because I have a prize to reach and a goal to achieve, and mostly because I have not reached that yet."

Our gaze has stayed too long on our own stumbles. The Spirit wants to shift our focus toward the goal line. Yes, you stumbled.

Yes, you took hits. That is not the end of the game. God points toward the prize, the upward call. He says, "Your pullback has been powerful. Now run. I am with you. My power sits behind your launch. The game is not finished. Go get it. Look forward. Press on... You win!"

I focus on this one thing: Forgetting the past and looking forward to what lies ahead, I press on to reach the end of the race and receive the heavenly prize for which God, through Christ Jesus, is calling us.
— Philippians 3:13-14 NLT

This is Paul saying: "I'm around 60 years old, I've seen, done and learned so much in life, but I am convinced that the things Jesus spoke of tells me THERE IS SO MUCH MORE. I want you to know I haven't even started yet. I'm going to keep PRESSING FORWARD until I lay hold of everything and more. I will not stop! I WILL NOT MISS MY TARGET! I WILL NOT SIN against God's plan for my life by missing this target set for me! I have this drive deep inside me. God is PROPELLING ME FORWARD until I reach the goal. I'm not after the prize. The prize will come automatically. It is the goal I am after. Hit the goal and you get the prize. That's how it works."

So many aim at prizes when they should be aiming at the goal... the target... the bullseye... the tryline!!! Get the Kingdom and everything else is added. Paul knew what he was aiming at.

May I remind you ... your destiny is to not let the devil get in your way. He will try, but that is not your reason to stop. When he does stand in your way, knock him down, push him to the side and keep running towards the goal of the upward call of God! Behind you stands Jesus, steady and unshaken. His left hand extends, pointing out the target - the upward call, the Kingdom purpose, the assignment prepared for you. With His right hand He draws back the bowstring that carries your life. None of this happens in random darkness. Heaven directs the shot. When His fingers release you, your life becomes an arrow of divine purpose no power of hell can stop mid-flight.

God is accelerating His people. Every new level on your journey carries a fresh launching moment. There is no shame in starting again. You may have started over more times than you ever planned. Heaven does not label that failure. Heaven counts every "yes" you give to God. Heaven honors those who finish, not those who never fall. Your Father looks for hearts that keep believing, keep repenting, keep getting up, keep obeying.

The enemy will try to stand in your way. That is not your cue to stop. Knock him down. Push him aside. Keep running. Many stand far closer to their finish line than they realize. The field looks long, yet Heaven says, "Look again. You are nearer than you thought." That nearness explains the intensity of the battle around you. Your next release out of the Lord's bow may become the one that moves you into everything for which you have paid such a high price. You are not stuck. You stand in a divine setup. The arrow is pulled back. A sudden change draws near.

Child of God, you are a powerful arrow in the Father's quiver. He is raising, aiming and readying many arrows in this hour, not for a doubtful battle, but for certain victory. The war's outcome has never been in question; the story of triumph simply has not reached its final chapter. Jesus handed the baton to His followers when He said, "As the Father has sent Me, I also send you." You carry that sending. You carry that victory DNA.

With God, every struggle turns into seed for testimony. No weapon formed in hell can prosper over a life held in His hand. Greater is the One within you than anything roaring in the world. In Christ you stand as more than a conqueror. Even when circumstances look backward, in Him you still move forward. Rowers sit facing the opposite direction, yet the boat slices ahead. That picture carries a word: do not judge your progress by sight alone.

When the enemy intends for harm, God turns it for good. If your situation does not yet carry the fragrance of "good," then the Author has not finished writing. You are called to live like an arrow: lean, focused, sharp, and surrendered. Let Him be the Archer.

I believe Heaven is saying, loud and clear: we are AIMED & READY. The last few years on this planet shook every system, exposed foundations and revealed hearts. Strange events on a global scale tried to drown hope. In the middle of all of that, God kept speaking. Prophetic words have been building like waves on the same ocean, connected and converging. Pullback for a season, yes. Abandonment, never. The God who starts a work completes it.

Right now, many sense heavy pushback in their spirit as they prepare to step out in faith to occupy promised territory. Do not panic. Rejoice. Tension on the line means release is close. What felt like a funeral in one season will prove to be a delivery room in the next. When Heaven calls for "COMEBACK," graves lose their grip, prodigals run home, captives taste freedom and barren places bloom again.

You stand in a holy hush. The bow is bent. The arrow is drawn. The Archer breathes out, steady and sure. At His fingertips sits your suddenly.

THE START OF A NEW BEGINNING

Every great move of God begins in a place that feels nothing like a beginning. It often arrives wearing the mask of loss, silence, burial or delay. Many divine turning points first appear as endings: chapters that look closed, seasons that seem stripped, landscapes that feel emptied of life. Yet Heaven holds a different view of these moments. God hides fresh beginnings inside places where sight sees decline, but faith can hear promise. What looks final to the human eye often stands as the doorway into something new, something rising, something Heaven has quietly prepared beneath the surface.

This has always been God's way. He shifts seasons with methods that run counter to natural instincts. When humans look for loud signals, God often works through quiet rearranging. When we look for open skies, He begins His movements underground. When we expect fireworks, He starts with seeds. When we search for movement, He releases a hush. In that hush, endings melt into beginnings, and what looked like collapse becomes the soil for resurrection.

We live in a world that evaluates progress through surface-level evidence: numbers, visibility, activity, and success. Heaven evaluates through alignment, surrender, timing and purpose.

God is never rushed by what we think is urgent. Nor is He hindered by landscapes that seem barren. He speaks "new" long before the ground shows signs of anything sprouting. He declares "forward" while we still feel held in place. He calls something alive while human reasoning sees no pulse. The Spirit keeps announcing newness because Heaven recognizes God's preparation long before the earth does.

This is the nature of divine beginnings: they rarely begin where we expect them.

UNDERSTANDING ZIGLAG -1 SAMUEL 30

Ziklag was a small, remote town tied to David during a season of deep exhaustion. David had spent years under pressure, leading people through constant danger while carrying responsibility he never asked for. He arrived in Ziklag searching for relief, rest and stability after a long stretch of survival. The town became a temporary place to breathe, regroup, and hold life together while the future remained uncertain. For a moment, Ziklag felt like a pause where life might finally settle. It was an in-between place where they could escape the things they've been through and not think about the battles still ahead.

That sense of stability shattered when an enemy group attacked the town while David and his men were away. Homes burned. Families were taken. Everything familiar vanished in a single blow. When David returned, Ziklag lay in ruins and grief overwhelmed everyone who stood there. The loss ran so deep that even David's closest supporters turned against him. In that moment of total collapse, with nothing left to lean on, David found the strength to rise again by turning inward and upward. What looked like the lowest point of his life became the turning point that led to recovery, restored purpose, and eventual leadership at a higher level.

Ziklag was a place where David never planned to remain, but it was good to take a break from running. It was never the destination promised over his life, never the throne he was anointed to occupy, and never the fulfillment he carried in his spirit. Ziklag existed as a temporary refuge during a prolonged season of pressure, pursuit, and exhaustion. It was a PULLBACK sanctuary. It was an in-between place. David arrived there carrying a God-given purpose while living in contradiction, holding a future crown while surviving in enemy territory. The tension of waiting had worn him down, and survival became louder than promise.

Ziklag represented a season shaped by fatigue. David had endured years of running, hiding, and leading under strain. Victory over Goliath sat in his past, while relentless opposition defined his present. Ziklag offered relief that looked practical but carried hidden cost. It was safety without destiny, shelter without alignment, and peace built on compromise. David stayed there long enough to believe stability had returned, until everything collapsed in a single devastating moment.

While David and his men were away offering aid to his hosts, Amalek attacked the city. Homes were destroyed. Families were taken. The place that once felt secure turned into ashes. When David returned, he walked into a scene so overwhelming that Scripture records his men weeping until their strength was gone. Ziklag became the moment where loss multiplied, grief deepened, and despair settled heavily on every heart. To the onlooker it must have looked hopeless, finished, buried and done.

The pressure intensified when the men turned on David. Pain twisted loyalty into accusation. The same warriors who followed him through caves and battlefields now spoke of taking his life. David stood alone, surrounded by devastation, abandoned by human strength, stripped of every visible support. Leadership felt heavier than ever, and the weight of responsibility pressed harder than the loss itself.

Ziklag reveals a sacred turning point because David responded differently than expected. Scripture says he strengthened himself in the Lord his God. In the ashes of loss, David reached upward. With no city to defend and no allies to rely on, he turned his focus toward the One who never shifted. Ziklag became the place where dependence deepened and clarity returned.

David sought the Lord and received direction. God instructed him to pursue, and David obeyed with renewed resolve. Recovery followed. Every stolen life returned. Every loss was restored. No one was missing. Ziklag transformed into a doorway rather than an ending. Shortly after this moment, David stepped into promotion and authority that had been delayed for years.

Ziklag carried purpose beyond pain. God was using it in ways David would only understand later. It stripped away false refuge and redirected David toward divine alignment. What burned revealed what never belonged in the future God had prepared. Ziklag dismantled survival mentality and awakened pursuit. It removed every illusion of control and replaced it with trust. The fire cleared space for advancement.

Ziklag moments still exist today. They appear during seasons when endurance runs thin and progress feels stalled. They arrive when accumulated pressure finally breaks open what seemed stable. Ziklag moments surface when leaders feel misunderstood, support fades, and loss compounds faster than answers. These moments feel deeply personal because they reach places where strength once lived.

A Ziklag moment marks the place when reliance shifts fully toward God. It becomes the point where clarity emerges after confusion, where courage rises after grief, where obedience replaces survival. Ziklag forces the heart to choose pursuit again. It demands alignment rather than retreat. It invites faith to stand tall even when surrounded by ruin.

David did not ascend to the throne apart from Ziklag. His leadership matured there. His trust solidified there. His obedience sharpened there. Ziklag became the soil where recovery was birthed and authority was strengthened. Fire refined him. Loss clarified him. Dependence anchored him.

When this book speaks of Ziklag moments, it speaks of seasons where everything familiar collapses while God prepares restoration. It points to moments when reduction becomes redirection and ashes give way to pursuit. Ziklag stands as evidence that devastation does not determine destiny. Alignment does.

If life feels reduced, scattered, or stripped bare, Ziklag may describe the season unfolding. That place does not signal abandonment. It signals preparation. Ziklag often stands immediately before recovery, promotion, and renewed purpose. The ashes do not speak the final word. God still does.

NEW BEGINNINGS DISGUISED AS ENDINGS

Scripture overflows with moments when Heaven hid a beginning under something that looked like an ending. Abraham saw barrenness; God saw a nation. Joseph endured betrayal, slavery and prison; God saw the shaping of a deliverer. Moses ran into the wilderness; God saw the making of a leader who would confront empires. Elijah hid beside a brook; God prepared a prophet who would call down fire. Israel spent decades in captivity; God saw a people ready to walk into promise.

The clearest example stands at the heart of our faith. The cross looked like finality. It looked like the end of hope, the shutting down of promise, the burial of every miracle Jesus performed. Yet the burial carried resurrection in its womb. Heaven announced victory while hell celebrated what it believed was defeat. This is the pattern of God: burial precedes power, endings usher in beginnings, and what looks lifeless becomes the cradle of new glory.

God still works this way. There are moments when you stand staring at a chapter that feels finished, dreams that feel delayed, prayers unanswered, relationships fractured, ministry stretched, resources tight, and strength worn thin. And yet, beneath all of that, God arranges something fresh. When you see an ending, He sees a reset. When you see silence, He sees preparation. When you see retreat, He sees positioning. When you see barren ground, He sees seeds pushing against the soil, ready to surge upward.

The whispers of the Spirit in this hour are loud and clear: "Don't confuse your promotion with your death". Many look at their circumstances and assume God has stepped back, yet the opposite often holds true. What feels like backward motion carries the potential for divine acceleration. Pullback precedes purpose because tension builds trajectory. What appears like loss can hide Heaven's windup. God uses these disguised moments to reroute, reshape and re-aim His people for what comes next.

RESURRECTION WRAPPED INSIDE BURIAL

Seeds tell this story better than words. You place them under the soil where no light reaches, and they disappear. Nothing about that moment feels promising. Many seeds wait underneath the earth for weeks, or even years, before anything breaks through. Yet under that layer of dirt, a miracle begins. Pressure, darkness and waiting forge the conditions for life. A seed's burial becomes its birthplace.

You walk through seasons exactly like that. Circumstances bury you under weight you did not expect. Dreams go quiet. Doors close. Momentum slows. You look at your life and see the stillness of winter. God sees the beginning of spring. The Spirit keeps announcing, *"New!"* while everything around you feels stuck because Heaven hears roots forming before leaves appear. Heaven celebrates fruit long before branches hold it.

"I believe so many of your seeds are about to burst forth with growth and so many of your trees will suddenly be covered in flowers," the word in your spirit keeps proclaiming. "Bare one moment, full the next!"

Nature preaches resurrection daily. A tree stripped naked by winter looks finished, yet within that same tree sap prepares to rise. Nobody sees it. Nobody hears it. But it climbs. Then suddenly one morning the branches hold color again. That sudden beauty is not random. It grew inside a season when everything looked motionless.

That is what resurrection feels like. A sudden shift that erupts out of a long quiet. A beginning wrapped inside a burial. A future that pushes through the very ground that once felt like loss. God has hidden beginnings for His people in places that seemed to fall apart. Your soil is not dead. It is pregnant.

NICO SMIT

GOD SHIFTS SEASONS WITH SILENCE, HIDDENNESS AND TENSION

Heaven is loud, but God's transitions are often quiet. He does His greatest work in silence. He moves pieces while no one is watching. He rearranges hearts, relationships, assignments and nations behind the curtain of hiddenness.

When the earth feels silent, Heaven is anything but inactive. Silence often signals that God is shaping you, strengthening you, and sharpening your aim. Hiddenness protects you while roots deepen. Tension equips you for greater distance. The bow bends before the arrow flies. The string tightens before release. Pullback prepares the arrow for an assignment it could never reach without pressure.

In your spirit, you may feel that tightness. That holy tension. Not anxiety, but alignment. Not fear, but formation. God uses tension to reveal what is strong, what is weak, what must break, what must stretch, what must mature. That stretch is not punishment; it is precision.

The church has been walking through this kind of tension. Many leaders sensed a global pullback, a strange heaviness, a season filled with trials and contradictions. Yet Heaven does not call it collapse. Heaven calls it windup, preparation, a Ziklag moment before recovery, a stretching before supernatural surge.

Seasons do not shift when circumstances look ready; they shift when God says, "Now." Silence is one of the clearest indicators that a shift is underway. Hiddenness becomes a womb for transformation. Tension becomes an arrow positioned on the bowstring of destiny.

FRUIT TREES AND FIELDS OF SEED: LIVING PARABLES OF NEWNESS

God wrote His nature into creation so that even the earth preaches His ways. Fruit trees, seeds, roots, vineyards, harvests—they speak the language of Heaven. They reveal the rhythm of God's heart: barren then bursting, quiet then flourishing, winter then spring. seedtime then harvest.

Fields ploughed bare do not look promising. Rows of dirt offer no evidence of what rests beneath. Yet a field holds more future than its appearance suggests. Under that soil seeds crack open, roots spread, life fights upward, and one day the same field that looked abandoned becomes thick with growth.

Trees give another picture. Their branches shed fruit, then leaves, then color. They endure frost, storms and long nights. But those branches still hold the memory of last season's harvest and the promise of the next. That memory sits in their structure. So, when warmth arrives, they respond with sudden abundance.

This is why creation does not panic in barren seasons. The orchard never cries out, "I must be dying!" The field never complains, "Nothing is happening!" They know the design. They understand the rhythm. They trust the cycle.

Yet God's people often panic in the very seasons that carry the most promise. We look at bare branches and assume failure. We see empty fields and assume nothing is working. We feel tension and assume God has stepped away.

He has not.

Everything in your life right now may look like the quiet part of the story. That is the perfect climate for new beginnings. God always starts in hidden places. He always prepares growth before He reveals it. He always stores power in roots before fruit appears.

Creation does not fear barrenness because it knows lush fruitfulness is coming. Heaven wants you to learn the same rhythm. Fruit waits for timing. Seeds wait for heat. Vision waits for fullness. There is no shame in looking barren for a moment when God has planted something inside you that will fill your future with abundance.

WHY THE SPIRIT ANNOUNCES "NEW" WHILE THE NATURAL LOOKS EMPTY

Every believer understands the frustration of hearing God speak "new thing," while nothing in life reflects it. He says *forward* while you stand still. He says *promotion* while you feel pressed. He says *rise* while your circumstances dip.

This is not contradiction. It is timing. Heaven speaks before the earth reveals. God calls things into existence before they appear. He declares shifts long before the landscape changes. The announcement comes before the evidence.

"Behold, I am doing a new thing! Now it springs up; do you not perceive it?"
— Isaiah 43:19

Notice what He asks: *Do you perceive it?* Not *do you see it?* Sight follows perception. Circumstances follow revelation. Every arrow must live in the future! God reveals a new thing before the natural world aligns with that revelation. Why? Because His voice creates the season. His word generates the future. His declaration sets direction even when the surroundings stay still.

This is why the Spirit keeps announcing newness. Heaven perceives what the natural cannot yet display. Heaven sees the curve of the bow, the readiness of the arrow, the primed moment before release. Heaven knows seeds have broken open beneath the soil. Heaven knows roots already stretch into new ground. Heaven knows the hush before movement.

In spiritual terms, emptiness is often the blank canvas God uses to paint beginnings. He clears space before He fills it. He dismantles old structures before releasing new wine. He quiets noise so His whisper can guide you. He removes supports that no longer serve your calling so you can stand on the grace appointed for this season.

When God says "new," He is revealing what Heaven has already seen. When the Spirit stirs that word in you, He is pulling back the curtain just enough for your faith to catch the direction of the Archer's aim.

Your life may feel empty right now, but Heaven says it holds promise. Your heart may feel quiet, but Heaven says it holds fire. Your path may feel paused, but Heaven says it holds momentum. You may feel buried, but Heaven says you hold resurrection.

You are standing at the start of a new beginning. Not because everything looks ready, but because the One who authors beginnings has whispered it over your life. God's declarations do not wait for ideal conditions. They create them. When He speaks newness, the old cannot stay. When He speaks life, death loses its claim. When He speaks resurrection, buried dreams stir beneath the soil.

Look not at what feels empty. Look at the One who holds your story. Look at the Archer who bends His bow. Look at the field that hides its harvest. Look at the tree preparing blossoms under winter bark.

Your beginning has already begun.

And soon, the earth around you will catch up to what Heaven has already announced.

THERE HAS TO BE A PULLBACK

Every arrow crafted for flight must endure a backward motion. No arrow moves forward until it has first been drawn back. No catapult launches until its arm strains under pressure. No rocket lifts until it trembles on the launchpad. Nothing in the Kingdom moves into destiny without a pullback. This is the design of God.

The pullback holds purpose - purpose you may not see at first. Purpose you may resist at times. Purpose that will not always feel holy yet, carries the fingerprint of Heaven. God uses backward motion to create forward impact. He uses hidden seasons to build unstoppable momentum. He uses tension to generate accuracy.

A pullback is not a penalty; it is preparation.

When you understand this, you stop fighting seasons that feel restrictive. You stop interpreting tension as rejection. You stop accusing yourself of failure when life tightens. You begin to see what Heaven sees: a divine setup forming behind the scenes.

NICO SMIT

PULLBACK IN GOD'S DESIGN: BOW, ARROW, CATAPULT, SEED, ROWER, ROCKET

Creation itself teaches this truth.

An archer never lifts a bow without knowing something must move backward before it can go forward. The bow curves under pressure. The string tightens. The arrow endures strain. None of it is random. Everything bends for the sake of distance. Everything tightens for the sake of accuracy. Everything pulls back for the sake of impact.

This image echoed through my spirit when the Lord revealed the arrow and the fully arched bow. The tension looked painful, the bow looked strained, the arrow looked uncomfortable. Yet Heaven said, "It's not what it looks like. The strain is the beginning, not the end. The pullback is why you will go far."

A catapult follows the same pattern. Ancient armies relied on a weapon that only released power after a deep windup. Soldiers would heave the mechanisms backward with all their strength. The entire frame would groan under the load. That backward motion signaled readiness. When the tension reached its limit, a single release sent massive stones soaring across the battlefield. Every enemy within range felt the force created by that pullback.

Seeds follow this pattern. They are pushed below ground. They experience pressure and darkness. Nothing in that early stage looks like potential. Yet the burial stage is essential. The seed splits. Roots push downward. Life awakens upward. Everything the seed becomes depends on what happens in that hidden pullback beneath the soil.

Rowers face backward, yet every stroke thrusts the boat forward. Life looks reversed, but motion is in the opposite direction. Their posture appears counterproductive, yet movement flows with strength.

Rockets showcase this design dramatically. Before lift-off, the ground shakes. The rocket trembles. Gravity fights for control. For a moment everything looks unstable. But that trembling is the signal that thrust is building. At full force, the rocket breaks free from restraint and rises with speed no human muscle could produce.

These images - bow, arrow, catapult, seed, rower, rocket, carry one lesson: backward motion in God's hands always precedes supernatural forward acceleration.

Nothing rises without a pullback.

> No one has ever won a game of chess by only taking forward moves. Sometimes you have to move backwards to take better steps forward. (Unknown)

TENSION BUILDS POWER; STRAIN CREATES POTENTIAL

If you feel stretched, tight, pressed or strained, it may be because Heaven is preparing distance and accuracy in your life.

The strain you feel does not reveal abandonment; it reveals assignment.

The Spirit is forming strength in the parts of you that must endure tension under the weight of calling. Tension strengthens resolve. Tension exposes what must be surrendered. Tension builds faith. Tension aligns direction. Without tension the arrow falls to the ground. Without the pull on the string, there is no velocity.

This is why the Lord said, "Don't over-focus on the strain - strength and cost it required to pull back the arrow."

The reason many are not 'walking on water' in their Christian life could be as simple as they are drawn to the winds and waves and not God. Look to Jesus... the author and finisher of our faith.

We look at discomfort and assume decline. God looks at discomfort and sees development. The place where you feel stretched is often the place where God is building capacity and power for destiny.

Strain is never pleasant, yet it carries holy purpose. The pullback season shapes character, corrects aim, purifies motives and deepens maturity. It generates endurance. It cultivates hunger. It clarifies priorities.

Most importantly: *tension proves what you trust.*

When life bends you backward, you discover who your Archer is. You learn to rely on His grip, His angle, His breath, His direction. You learn stillness. You learn surrender. You learn to resist the urge to leap from His hand too soon.

The moment of greatest tension often becomes the moment of greatest accuracy.

Promotion in the Kingdom rarely feels like elevation. The initial experience often feels more like burial, reduction, stripping, pruning—anything but increase.

It is common to misinterpret the signs. You pray for expansion, then find yourself in a smaller place. You pray for breakthrough, then walk into a valley. You pray for influence, then experience isolation. You pray for clarity, then endure confusion. You pray for harvest, then step into drought.

Yet Heaven views these moments as essential. A seed must go down before it rises. A soldier must train in hidden places before he stands on a battlefield. A prophet must grow in silence before he speaks with weight. A leader must be refined before carrying authority. The goodness of God will never exalt anyone without a foundation strong enough to bear the full weight of glory such an assignment would bring.

This is why promotion often feels like death, because old identities, old habits, old fears, old ways of moving must be laid down so new strength can rise. What feels like loss is sometimes God removing what cannot travel into the next season. What feels like backward movement is God rewiring the heart for forward assignment.

Promotion is rarely comfortable. But comfort never created warriors, reformers, prophets, apostles or revivalists.

God promotes His people by preparing them. Preparation is pressure. Pressure is pullback.

When the Lord said, "Your release is imminent," He did not mean comfort was imminent. He meant purpose was.

Many saints mistake this preparation season for decline because the sensation of pullback can mimic the feeling of failure. Yet Heaven sees a different picture. Heaven sees the bow drawn tight. Heaven sees the arrow steady. Heaven sees distance forming.

Promotion often begins in the very place where you feel least qualified, least visible or least confident. God promotes those willing to endure His shaping, not those seeking their own spotlight.

If it feels like death, it may be because resurrection stands next in line.

PERSONAL, CORPORATE AND GLOBAL PULLBACK SEASONS

Pullback does not only touch individuals. It touches families, ministries, churches, cities and even nations. Heaven applies this pattern broadly because it is a Kingdom law.

Personal Pullbacks

On a personal level, pullback seasons can manifest as emotional heaviness, spiritual dryness, relational strain, financial pressure or unexpected obstacles. These moments confront the deepest questions of purpose. They strip away false strength. They expose whether your confidence sits in Christ or in circumstances.

Many believers who walk through intense personal pullbacks later discover that the season prepared them to carry authority they could not have held earlier. The pullback built resilience. It sharpened discernment. It activated intercession. It stirred hunger that comfort never could.

After all, is the story of the Prodigal Son's pullback and comeback not a great example of what God can do when we get down to just Him and us?

Corporate Pullbacks

Churches, ministries and movements also experience collective pullback. We saw this in recent years as congregations worldwide faced unprecedented strain. Attendance fluctuated. Structures shifted. Leaders faced pressure. Many communities mourned loss, confusion and uncertainty.

Yet prophetic voices around the globe kept hearing the same message: *This is not retreat; it is windup.*

Churches that appeared smaller were being sharpened. Churches that felt quieter were being refined. Churches that walked through spiritual drought were being pruned for greater capacity. God has been preparing His people for a surge of harvest, new wine and fresh oil.

This is why the Spirit says new wineskins are essential. Old systems cannot hold what Heaven plans to pour out. The season of tightening and stretching is essential for expansion.

Global Pullbacks

Nations have felt the tremors of global pullback. Political instability, cultural upheaval, moral confusion, spiritual warfare - these are not random waves of chaos. They reveal spiritual pressure accumulating across the earth, preparing for a release of God's presence unlike anything seen in modern history.

The last five years carried a global pullback. A worldwide hush. A season that exposed idols, shook institutions, tested faith, and re-aimed the church. God has been aligning His people across continents for a coordinated comeback - one that impacts nations, harvest fields and generations.

Heaven has not been silent. Heaven has been aiming.

WHY MANY MISREAD WARFARE FOR FAILURE

When tension rises, warfare increases. When warfare increases, many mistake it for personal failure. Yet warfare is often the clearest sign that Heaven is positioning you.

The enemy does not waste ammunition on those going nowhere. The enemy fights those being pulled back into God's purpose.

He fights those being refined for accuracy. He fights those being aimed at territory he has occupied for too long.

This is why the war intensifies right before release.

Warfare can feel like confusion, discouragement, heaviness, fatigue or spiritual fog. But its timing exposes its purpose. The enemy knows when you are close to breakthrough. He senses tension on the bow. He sees the angle of Heaven's aim. He recognizes the moment you are about to strike what he hoped would stand untouched.

Many saints interpret warfare as evidence they did something wrong. Heaven sees warfare as evidence they are drawing near to what is right.

This is why the Spirit said, "Don't aim at the devil. Aim at My glory."

If you aim at the devil, you lose focus. If you aim at Jesus, you gain victory.

Warfare wants to shift your gaze. Pullback wants to refine your gaze. God wants to fix your gaze.

The Archer does not allow warfare to derail what He has prepared. He uses it to sharpen awareness, strengthen endurance and deepen dependency. Resistance becomes training ground. Pressure becomes holy preparation.

When you learn to interpret warfare correctly, you stop retreating. You stop spiraling into discouragement. You stop misreading your season. You begin to stand in confidence, knowing Heaven wastes nothing, not even the attacks of hell.

Warfare can shout loudly. But the Archer speaks louder.

AIMED & READY

PULLBACK REVEALS THE ARCHER'S HAND

The most important part of pullback is not the tension. It is the hand that holds you.

Behind every arrow stands a skilled archer. One who knows how far to pull. One who knows how long to hold. One who knows the exact moment to release. One who knows which target requires your flight.

You are not bending under random pressure. You are bending under divine direction.

Pullback reveals trust. It reveals whether you believe the Archer knows what He is doing. It reveals whether you believe He chooses your target with precision. It reveals whether you rest in His grip.

This season may stretch you. It may confuse you. It may challenge everything in you. But it is shaping you for accuracy you could not reach otherwise.

The Archer does not miss.

DID YOU KNOW SIN IS MISSING THE BULLSEYE?

Your life has divine purpose all over it. That's why sin is a diversion from God's best. God does not want you to miss. He intends for you to hit the mark and succeed. Maybe you forgot that the word for "sin" actually means falling short of its intended target. It comes from the Hebrew words *chattaahor chata*. God has no desire that any of His children miss the mark.

He is pulling you back because distance matters for what comes next. Accuracy matters. Impact matters. Purpose matters.

There has to be a pullback because without it, you would never reach the assignment prepared for you.

There has to be a pullback because Heaven always moves through pressure before it moves through power.

There has to be a pullback because you are being shaped into a weapon of purpose.

There has to be a pullback because you are being aimed at something significant.

There has to be a pullback because you are meant to strike deep.

You are not misaligned. You are not forgotten. You are not failing. You are not weakening.

You are being drawn, and Heaven is getting ready to release you.

BE STILL: IT'S A HOLY HUSH

Before every divine movement comes a moment when Heaven quiets the atmosphere. A stillness enters the soul so deep it almost feels unnatural. Conversations soften. Opportunities pause. Familiar rhythms slow. Even prayers shift tone, filled with less striving and more listening. That silence is not absence or defeat. It is not inactivity. It is a holy hush. A sacred pause engineered by the Archer Himself because stillness makes aiming accurate.

Be still, and know that I am God
— Psalm 46:10

It is important to know that the psalmist penned these words during a time of great noise and disaster not during the serene quietness most imagine it to be! The Hebrew word for 'BE STILL' means: 'Stop resisting or fighting, calm down, and believe'. In Aramaic it means: 'Stop. Repent and change how you're thinking!' The psalmist is talking about learning how to completely trust God in every moment. This 'BE STILL' asks a truly significant question: Do you know He is God! Do you believe it? Then slow down your panic, put to rest your fears and trust Him to be God in your world.

He was in the stern, asleep on a pillow. And they awoke Him and said to Him, "Teacher, do You not care that we are perishing?" Then He arose and rebuked the wind, and said to the sea, PEACE, BE STILL! And the wind ceased and there was a great calm. But He said to them, "WHY ARE YOU SO FEARFUL? HOW IS IT THAT YOU HAVE NO FAITH?"
— Mark 4:38-40 (emphasis mine)

The word used here for 'BE STILL' is also the word hush. When Jesus spoke this word, He was reminding the winds and the waves that they are under the authority of God. The arrows had a mission to complete. So, Jesus drew from the heavenly peace inside Him to make still the world around Him. Shhh ... God is about to release His arrows.

Every believer who walks closely with God will eventually encounter this hush. It is the moment right before release, the breath between aim and impact, the still point where Heaven positions you with precision. This hush carries strategy for the season ahead. It is not wasted time; it is divine timing. It is one of the most holy privileges we get.

If the pullback prepares your strength, the hush prepares your accuracy.

THE PROPHETIC HUSH BEFORE RELEASE

When the Archer draws the bow, tension increases until the arrow reaches its furthest point back. In that final moment He stops completely. No shaking. No rushing. No hesitation. His breath steadies. His focus narrows. Everything goes quiet. That quiet contains the transition between forming and launching.

Heaven uses the same pattern with His people.

There comes a moment when God says, *"Still yourself. Remain in place. Pay attention. Every distraction must be silenced so you do not miss what I am preparing to do next."* In that hush, nothing moves on the outside, but everything shifts on the inside. God refines sight, aligns motives, closes unnecessary doors, and awakens deeper discernment.

The hush is the chamber where clarity meets assignment.

This is why the Spirit cautions: *"Don't miss this holy hush. You're not stuck, you're building power and generating momentum for My yes and amen promises."*

The hush is not punishment; it is invitation. It is a call into sensitivity. A call into rest. A call into alignment. Heaven speaks in whispers at times because whispers force you to draw near.

The greatest revelations often arrive in quiet rooms, not public stages.

The greatest strategies often come during still nights, not crowded days.

The greatest breakthroughs often begin when you hear God say, *"Stop. Wait. Hold. Let Me finish aiming you."*

The hush carries weight and wonder. It is the soundless stage where destiny gets its final adjustments.

THE ARCHER'S PAUSE — PRECISION, BREATH, SILENCE

Archers know this truth: the pause is as essential as the pullback. The arrow never launches while the archer is in motion. Movement disrupts accuracy. Rushing destabilizes aim. Fidgeting sabotages impact.

In warfare, archers learned to quiet their breath and still their bodies to achieve maximum precision. The release did not depend solely on strength; it depended on control. A skilled archer mastered the ability to freeze in the exact moment tension reached perfection.

This imagery mirrors the spiritual posture God invites us to embrace.

When He has pulled you back far, He brings you into stillness so that divine breath can steady your aim. That stillness holds purpose:

Precision. God aligns your heart with His target.
Perspective. You see what matters and what no longer does.
Purity. Motives become clear.
Peace. Fear loses ground.
Positioning. You rest exactly where God wants you before He releases you.

The hush is not empty space. It is alignment space.

That is why rushing feels dangerous in this season. Moving ahead prematurely will always cause the arrow to miss the mark. Many believers pray for acceleration, yet the Archer knows that momentum with poor aim is a liability. He stills His people, so their next step carries Kingdom accuracy.

The hush is mercy. It is the breath before breakthrough.

STILLNESS AS THE PLACE OF DIVINE STRATEGY

Stillness in God's Kingdom does not mean inactivity. It means clarity. It means surrender to divine timing. It means listening long enough to hear the next instruction.

God often withdraws His people into still places before He thrusts them into significant assignment. Jesus withdrew into mountains and solitary fields before healing masses, confronting demons, revealing Kingdom mysteries, or raising the dead. His power flowed from His stillness.

Stillness is where divine strategy forms.

When everything around you goes quiet, God is releasing renewed sharpness. This sharpening cannot happen in chaos. Quiet is God's tool to carve out wisdom. Silence becomes a sanctuary where agendas fall away and priorities reorder.

In stillness, you discover:

- what to pick up and what to drop
- what to pursue and what to ignore
- what is God's direction and what is distraction
- what is timely and what is premature

Many believers fear stillness because it confronts their inner noise. Yet the hush is essential for Kingdom accuracy. It clears the fog. It returns you to simplicity. It releases discernment that gets buried under busyness.

Stillness slows the world long enough for God's strategy to rise.

When God says, *"Be still,"* He is positioning you to receive something you could not perceive until you stopped moving.

BETWEEN MALACHI AND MATTHEW: THE 400-YEAR HUSH

One of the greatest examples of divine silence sits between the final prophet of the Old Testament and the arrival of Jesus in the New. Malachi closes, the ink dries, and Heaven goes quiet. Generations pass. No angelic visitations. No thunderous prophetic declarations. No new writings. The silence stretches across four centuries.

To human eyes, it may have looked as though God stepped away. Yet Heaven was not idle. That long quiet contained the shaping of nations, the rise and fall of empires, the building of roads, the spreading of languages, and the lining up of world conditions that would cradle the birth of the Messiah. That hush prepared the world for Heaven's Arrow, Jesus, sent to strike the bullseye of redemption.

It was God weaving history into perfect alignment so that when Jesus stepped into the world, every prophecy converged, every promise found its stage, and every shadow met its substance.

There was such a HUSH between Malachi and Matthew - 400 years when it looked like nothing was happening, but it was the pullback for heaven's mightiest arrow.

When God introduces stillness, He is placing everything into perfect order. Heaven prepares launches with far more strategy than we realize. What feels like inactivity to us is intense preparation in the spirit realm.

God's silence is never empty. His silence is full.

Full of purpose.
Full of alignment.
Full of strength.
Full of hidden activity.
Full of the next move.

Malachi to Matthew shows us what many believers forget: the hush precedes the greatest releases of God.

WHY EVERYTHING GETS QUIET RIGHT BEFORE EVERYTHING MOVES FAST

Divine acceleration often begins in the quietest season of your life. That quiet does not mean weakening; it means tightening. It means final adjustments. It means last-minute realignment so that when the moment arrives, your launch carries maximum impact.

The hush before release is a mark of divine timing.

Think of the final seconds before a rocket lifts from the launchpad. Engineers hold their breath. Systems go silent. Instruments lock into their final readings. A countdown whispers through the speakers. Nothing seems to move, yet everything is seconds away from violent acceleration. That stillness is essential because once the engines ignite, there is no turning back.

So it is with Heaven.

There comes a point in your spiritual journey where things go quiet, not because you are losing momentum but because you are about to gain more than you can imagine. Everything in your life begins to simplify. Desires rearrange. Noise loses its grip. You feel God's hand steadying you. You feel the pressure of divine focus. You sense movement under the surface, though nothing has manifested yet.

This is the holy hush.

It is the pause before the suddenly.
It is the breath before the release.
It is the quiet before spiritual velocity.

The Archer's fingers hold the string at full tension. The arrow rests still, though every fiber of its being knows it is seconds away from flight.

Right now, we are in a prophetic hush. The arrow and the string are resting fully on the fingertips of God.

Heaven's timing is precise. God does not release His people while their focus wavers. He releases them when everything inside them matches the target ahead. The hush trains your soul to recognize His aim. It protects you from stepping outside His will. It ensures that when movement comes, it comes with unstoppable force.

Many saints fear quiet seasons because they misunderstand them. They associate silence with distance. They think nothing is happening. They assume God is no longer active. Yet the quietest moments often hold the most intense spiritual construction.

Heaven quiets you to accelerate you.

Heaven slows you to prepare you.

Heaven empties noise to fill you with instruction.

Heaven hushes the world so you can hear the whisper that births the next season of your destiny.

The hush is the beginning of targeted momentum.

THE HUSH PROTECTS YOU FROM PREMATURE RELEASE

One of the most dangerous things that can happen to a believer is leaving the Archer's hand too early. Many arrows fly prematurely, not because they are rebellious, but because they are impatient. They feel the tension and assume it means time to move. But tension alone is not the signal; the release belongs to the Archer.

If the arrow leaves the hand prematurely, it misses its mark. If it refuses the aim of the Archer, it becomes useless.

The hush protects you from wasted impact.

It prevents you from stepping through doors that are not yours.

It guards you from partnerships that dilute your calling.

It shields you from distractions that would fracture your focus.

It preserves your strength for the assignment chosen for you.

Premature release always leads to exhaustion, confusion and unnecessary warfare. Right timing leads to effortless impact.

The hush teaches you that your destiny does not rely on your pace but rather on your posture. God wants your willingness, not your rushing.

The hush teaches trust.
The hush teaches patience.
The hush teaches that movement must come from God to carry God's results.

Authority is never gained in noisy places. Authority is born in stillness. Those who learn to be quiet before God carry weight when they speak. Those who listen deeply hear what others miss. Those who wait learn to recognize Heaven's rhythm.

The prophets learned this. Kings learned this. Apostles learned this. Jesus embodied this.

Authority grows in seasons where voices fall silent and God's whisper fills the space.

If you feel hidden, you are being entrusted with depth. If you feel stilled, you are being trusted with precision. If you feel silenced, you are being prepared to speak with greater authority.

Stillness matures you for what noise cannot teach. It prepares your heart for impact.

LEARNING TO TRUST THE HUSH

To embrace the hush, you must resist the instinct to manufacture movement. You must resist the fear that says something must be wrong. You must resist the pressure to prove yourself, defend yourself or push yourself prematurely.

The hush requires surrender.
Surrender to divine timing.
Surrender to God's aim.
Surrender to the wisdom of the Archer.

This hush is active faith, even when it feels passive. It is intentional quiet. It is choosing to rest in the place between God's fingers and your future.

Never forget that you are held, positioned, and focused. When the Archer steadies His hands, you steady your spirit. When the

Archer breathes deeply, you breathe with Him. When the Archer holds the pause, you hold it with Him.

This hush is holy. This hush is necessary. This hush is filled with promise.

You are being prepared for speed, accuracy and impact you have never known before. The hush will not last forever. But while it lasts, let it shape you. Let it still you. Let it settle you into God's perfect aim.

Soon His fingers will open, and the world will witness what Heaven prepared in silence.

YOU'RE IN AN IN-BETWEEN PLACE

Jesus said: Let's go over to the other side
— Mark 4:35

Jesus said nothing about the journey or what was waiting for them. When we choose to follow Jesus and go on a journey with Him, He knows what we are going to face. When Jesus said: Let us go!... It's a powerful promise. He didn't say: 'Let's go to the middle of the Sea of Galilee and drown.' Jesus didn't promise smooth sailing, but He did promise a safe passage. It was so powerful that Jesus could sleep through the journey! Jesus knew their arrival had a guarantee connected to it. He knew God loves to work in the in-between places. The places between where you are and where He is aiming you.

Every believer walks through a stretch of life that sits between what God promised and what God will manifest. This space rarely feels glorious. It often carries ache, longing, tension and mystery. It is the zone where your faith grows louder than your sight. It is the landscape between prophecy and fulfillment, calling and arrival, declaration and demonstration. God's Word calls places like this "wilderness," "waiting," "sojourning," "testing," "journeying". Heaven sees them as formation grounds.

It is the ground where trust matures, motives solidify, and identity takes root. It is where God brings you low enough to hear His whisper and steady enough to recognize His hand. It is where He removes the rush of self-effort and reveals the inner strength you will need when the promise unfolds.

Every great biblical figure experienced this space, and every believer who carries Kingdom purpose will walk through it too. The in-between place is sacred, even when it feels uncomfortable.

The ache of waiting can feel sharper than warfare. Warfare energizes while waiting empties. Warfare stirs your spirit while waiting stretches it. Warfare demands action while waiting demands surrender. In all of these cases, it is challenging to live in the in-between.

It is in the in-between where many cry out:
"Lord, You spoke, so why hasn't it happened yet?"
"I know You called me, so why does everything feel paused?"
"I believed Your word, so why is life so still?"

This ache is evidence that your spirit has already glimpsed something your circumstances have not caught up with yet. The ache forms when your internal world shifts before your external world does.

Abraham lived inside this tension for decades. David sat inside it while waiting for the throne he was anointed for. Joseph endured it in prison while carrying a dream meant for nations. Hannah prayed through it. Moses fled into it. Israel wandered through it.

Your life carries a similar ache because Heaven has placed destiny inside you that does not fit your current surroundings.

This ache is not your enemy. It signals that divine promise is alive!

Waiting becomes painful when the seed within begins to swell. The ache reveals growth the same way pressure in a seed reveals germination. Something is expanding inside you even if nothing appears above ground yet.

Waiting hurts because growth is happening.

DELAYS AS DIVINE MERCY SHAPING READINESS

Delay can feel cruel when you want nothing more than forward motion. Yet Heaven often hides mercy inside delay.

Delay keeps you from stepping into rooms that aren't prepared for your arrival.
Delay keeps you from launching into assignments that require maturity you haven't yet developed.
Delay protects you from battles you are not yet equipped to win.
Delay ensures that when you rise, you rise with grace, depth, conviction and staying power.

Many people fear delay because they equate it with denial. But God uses delay as a tool of love, not frustration.

Delay is how God shapes readiness.

People often assume they are prepared simply because they desire something. Desire is not readiness. Desire can be pure, but readiness requires structure. Readiness requires endurance.

Readiness requires weight-bearing capacity. Readiness requires a surrendered heart that can carry influence with humility.

You may want the promise now; God wants you to last long after the promise arrives.

This is mercy.

Divine delay is not God withholding your future—it is God fortifying it.

When the Lord spoke through your spirit that "the release is pain-free, but the pullback takes much effort,"
He was revealing this truth: the hard part of destiny happens before the moment of movement.

Once you finally fly, momentum will feel effortless. But God will not compromise preparation to satisfy impatience. He loves you too much to release you unready.

Here's a truth you need to remember in every moment: Delay is not lost time. It is *invested* time.

WILDERNESS SEASONS WHERE MANNA STILL ARRIVES, YET IT IS NOT THE FINAL HOME

The in-between place often resembles the wilderness Israel walked through after leaving Egypt. They were free, yet not settled. Redeemed, yet not rooted. Chosen, yet not positioned. Led, yet not arrived. Fed daily, yet still longing for the land promised to them.

The wilderness is a strange place because it contains both miracle and monotony.

Manna comes every morning, proving God's nearness.
But manna also reminds you that you are not yet home.

Cloud and fire guide you, proving His leadership.
But the guiding reveals how far the journey still stretches.

Water flows from rocks, proving His power.
Yet the landscape stays barren, proving this is not the destination.

This tension confuses many believers. They experience God's faithfulness but not fullness. They see provision but not promise. They receive direction but not completion. They feel God sustaining them, but not yet planting them.

Yet wilderness seasons are essential. They purge Egypt from Israel's memory. They train hearts to rely on God rather than bondage, memory or fear. They dismantle cycles of insecurity and teach rhythms of trust. They transform former slaves into future inheritors.

The wilderness is a place of transformation, and manna is proof of God's patience, not of His delay. Manna is God saying, *"You are not where you will be, but you are not where you were. I am with you in the stretch."*

Every believer experiences this kind of wilderness at least once. Many experience it several times. Each wilderness marks a transition. It may feel like an ending, but it is truly a bridge.

WHY WANDERING DOES NOT EQUAL LOST

One of the greatest lies the enemy whispers during in-between seasons is that wandering equals being lost. But wandering and lost are not the same thing.

Lost means no direction.
Wandering means you are on a journey.

Lost means alone.
Wandering means guided, albeit slowly.

Lost means abandoned.
Wandering means held.

Israel wandered, but they were never lost.
Cloud by day, fire by night.
Manna from Heaven.
Water from unexpected places.
Victories against impossible enemies.

God never left them. He formed them through their wandering.

The in-between place often creates the illusion of wandering because progress appears slow. You do not see milestones. You do not feel momentum. You do not hold evidence of forward motion. Yet Heaven sees differently.

When God leads, wandering becomes preparation.
When God leads, wandering becomes refinement.
When God leads, wandering becomes repositioning.
When God leads, wandering becomes the road to destiny.

Some paths are straight. Others wind. Some move quickly. Others take time. But the shape of the journey does not determine the certainty of the destination.

You are not lost simply because you cannot yet see the finish line. Sometimes God hides the finish line, so you focus on His voice.

He guides one step at a time, so you learn dependence.
He reveals one instruction at a time, so you cultivate listening.

He opens one door at a time, so you grow content with His pace. He lifts one burden at a time, so you recognize His strength, not your own.

The enemy tries to convince you that wandering means failure. But wandering can be the clearest sign that you are in God's process. You are not retreating; you are moving through terrain that shapes your ability to carry what comes next.

Even Jesus spent time in the wilderness before stepping into His full public ministry. His wandering prepared Him for authority. It sharpened His identity. It revealed the Father's voice in ways crowds never could.

If Jesus walked through an in-between place, why should we fear ours?

THE IN-BETWEEN PLACE PRODUCES ENDURANCE

You gain something in the in-between that you cannot gain anywhere else: endurance.

Endurance cannot be imparted; it must be developed.
Endurance cannot be bought; it must be lived.
Endurance cannot be microwaved; it must be forged.

Nothing strengthens your spirit like trusting God without visible evidence. Nothing deepens your faith like believing when the landscape looks unchanged. Nothing matures your walk like choosing obedience in seasons where the reward is not yet visible.

God loves you too much to give you a calling you cannot endure. He trains your endurance in the in-between place, so when you step into promise, you remain standing.

Endurance prevents collapse under blessing.
Endurance prevents compromise under pressure.
Endurance prevents distraction under opportunity.
Endurance prevents giving up when responsibilities multiply.

The promise requires endurance. The in-between builds it.

THE BEAUTY HIDDEN IN THE LIMINAL SPACE

Liminal spaces, those transitional zones where old has passed but new has not fully formed, often feel uncomfortable, yet they carry treasures:

- **Clarity** you could not find in the noise of previous seasons
- **Humility** shaped when answers do not come quickly
- **Hunger** birthed when comfort no longer satisfies
- **Focus** sharpened when all unnecessary weight falls away
- **Revelation** only found in slow, quiet obedience
- **Resilience** that cannot be formed in ease

This is the hour where God is reminding His people:
"You are closer than you think. What feels like wandering is alignment. What feels like delay is shaping. What feels like pause is preparation."

You are not circling aimlessly.
You are being positioned.
The cloud is still above you.
The fire is still in front of you.
The Archer's hand is still steady.

You are held between promise and fulfillment, exactly where Heaven wants you. The in-between place.

AIMED & READY

"I am certain that God, who began the good work within you, will continue his work until it is finally finished."
— Philippians 1:6

Soon the Archer's fingers will open.
Soon the promise will rise.
Soon what felt slow will move with speed.

But for now...
Trust the hush.
Honor the pullback.
Embrace the wilderness.
Follow the cloud.
Collect the manna.
Strengthen your spirit.
Steady your aim.

You are in an in-between place, and that means God is getting you ready for arrival.

PART II: THE HAND OF THE ARCHER

CHAPTER 5

ARE YOU READY FOR WHAT'S COMING?

Across the earth right now, something is shifting with unmistakable intensity. You can feel it in prayer rooms, in worship gatherings, in late-night intercession, and in moments when the Spirit interrupts your ordinary day. Heaven is accelerating the pace of God's work among His people, and the atmosphere carries a sense of divine urgency unlike previous seasons. The shaking in nations, the hunger rising in churches, the stirring in the hearts of believers, all point toward one reality: God is preparing to release His arrows. The question is no longer whether Heaven is moving. The real question is whether God's people are ready for what comes next.

Acceleration in the Kingdom does not resemble the frantic speed of human effort. Heaven's acceleration feels like weight settling into purpose, vision sharpening, distractions falling away, and a deep internal readiness forming long before outward movement becomes visible. Many have sensed this for months, even years:

time feels compressed, seasons shift more rapidly, and the Spirit speaks with heightened clarity. What once took years appears to unfold in weeks. What once required repeated confirmations now arrives with single-sentence direction. God is moving swiftly because the harvest is ripe, the nations are thirsty, and generations have reached a tipping point where Heaven's intervention is both necessary and imminent.

This acceleration does not mean chaos; it means alignment. When Heaven accelerates, clarity comes with it. People who once struggled to discern direction now sense an unmistakable pull. Leaders who wrestled with uncertainty now realize God has been preparing them for a decisive moment. Churches that lived through pruning seasons now feel the stirring of new wine. Believers who endured long stretches of stillness now perceive the ground trembling beneath their feet, signaling the beginning of divine momentum. Heaven accelerates when the Archer has finished aiming.

But before Heaven releases acceleration, Heaven shakes the earth. Scripture reveals this pattern repeatedly. God shook Egypt before delivering Israel. God shook Midian's oppression before raising Gideon. God shook the religious landscape before Jesus stepped into public ministry. God shook the early church with wind and fire before sending them into all nations. Global shaking is never random; it signals that God's hand is drawing the bowstring close to its release point.

The shaking we have witnessed in recent years - cultural confusion, economic instability, worldwide fear, spiritual polarization, moral upheaval - has not been a sign of abandonment. It has been a sign of alignment. The world is not spiraling out of control. The world is being positioned for awakening. Heaven has been stirring underneath the surface while humanity has watched systems tremble. That trembling is not the end of hope. It is the signal that Heaven's arrows are about to be released with force and clarity.

Global turbulence has not meant the church is retreating, it has meant the church is winding up, preparing for a surge of movement shaped by the hand of God Himself. Many believers have been misreading the atmosphere because the shaking feels uncomfortable. Yet discomfort does not contradict divine purpose. Discomfort often reveals that Heaven is pressing close. God does not shake the earth to destroy His people. He shakes the earth so that everything anchored in the temporary falls away, leaving only what can carry eternal weight. This shaking, uncomfortable as it has been, has created the perfect conditions for release.

As Heaven accelerates activity in the earth, many have begun feeling something they struggle to articulate: a spiritual "push back" in their inner world. It is the sensation of pressure increasing, not because you are moving backward, but because you are approaching the breaking point of a launch. A rocket feels the greatest resistance moments before liftoff. Rowers feel the strongest backward pull moments before their boat cuts forward. Seeds feel the tightest confines moments before they break through the soil. In the same way, believers feel the heaviest spiritual tension right before God thrusts them into their next assignment.

This pushback is not a sign of regression; it is a sign that you are nearing release. Heaven often allows pressure to intensify so that your spirit becomes fully alert to what is unfolding. Many have wondered why NOW feels heavier, tighter or more spiritually intense than previous seasons. The answer is simple: you are standing on God's launchpad. Your life has reached an intersection where past obedience meets future purpose, where hidden preparation meets public assignment, where internal transformation meets external acceleration. Heaven applies pressure only when Heaven is ready to propel.

When the Lord showed me the image of the arrow under pressure, bow bent, arrow resting in tension, He revealed that what looks like strain is often the final stage before movement. The spiritual pushback people feel is not meant to discourage; it is meant to alert them: *"Get ready. Your release is near. The Archer's hand is steady. The hush is ending. The flight is about to begin."*

This moment on God's launchpad carries unique characteristics, and discerning them helps believers recognize their place in Heaven's timeline. One key marker is **sensitivity**. When God is preparing to release someone, their spiritual senses sharpen. They hear God more clearly. They feel conviction more quickly. They awaken earlier in the morning with a weight they cannot ignore. Worship becomes deeper, Scripture becomes more alive, and prayer feels less like discipline and more like breathing. The Spirit heightens awareness because accuracy matters once the arrow leaves the Archer's hand.

Another marker is **restlessness**. Not the restless anxiety of fear, but the restlessness of spiritual readiness. You sense you cannot remain where you are. Something inside you knows the ground beneath your feet will not be your landing spot. You recognize that old rhythms do not fit anymore. Old habits feel too small. Old surroundings feel temporary. Old mindsets feel outdated. This restlessness is spiritual labor. Just as a woman approaches the moment of birth with a deep knowledge that change is imminent, so the spirit senses when Heaven is preparing release.

A third marker is **holy dissatisfaction**. When you are on God's launchpad, you cannot settle for old wine. You cannot be satisfied with stagnant faith. You cannot remain comfortable in spiritual autopilot. Everything in you begins to hunger for more of God's presence, more clarity, more purity, more courage. Holy dissatisfaction is the fuel Heaven uses to ensure that once you are launched, you pursue purpose with conviction rather than coasting on convenience.

Then comes the marker that catches many by surprise: **increased spiritual resistance**. When the enemy senses that Heaven is positioning someone for significant impact, he attempts to cloud perception, disrupt confidence and distort identity. Warfare intensifies not because you are vulnerable, but because you are valuable. You are being placed on a trajectory meant to strike areas the enemy has guarded fiercely. He attacks most fiercely when you are closest to breakthrough. Recognizing this changes how you interpret resistance. Instead of seeing it as a threat, you begin to see it as confirmation: *"I am in position. God is aiming me. Heaven sees distance ahead of me."*

AIM WHERE YOU'RE GOING, NOT WHERE YOU ARE

Something interesting I learned recently is about how scientists plot a rockets course. If you want to launch a rocket to the moon, you don't aim for where it is, but to where it is going to be. If you aimed at where it is now, you would miss it, because by the time the rocket gets to where the moon is it had already moved on. This is why we need to trust God in where He aims our lives. He is not aiming at what has been, but what will be. He makes sure that by the time the arrow reaches its bullseye it is where it needs to be.

To be ready for what is coming, believers must embrace a posture of spiritual alertness. Heaven is not calling for frantic activity. Heaven is calling for awakened attention. You ready yourself not by running ahead, but by remaining sensitively aligned with the Archer's grip. God does not release arrows that resist His aim. He releases arrows that yield.

This means readiness begins with surrender. Surrender of timing, surrender of expectations, surrender of past disappointments, surrender of self-driven agendas. When you surrender, God adjusts your direction. When you surrender, God protects you from premature movement. When you surrender, God aligns your heart with His target. Readiness is not about anticipating your own plan; it is about attuning your spirit to His plan.

Readiness also carries courage. Heaven does not release arrows into shallow battles. God sends His people into territory that requires boldness, conviction and spiritual resilience. The assignments coming in this next season will not be small. They will not be casual. They will carry weight for cities, families, churches and even nations. Heaven is looking for those willing to step into places that demand supernatural dependence. Your readiness is measured not by your comfort level but by your willingness to obey.

There is another layer to readiness - joy. Not superficial emotion, but the deep, steady joy that comes from recognizing you are part of Heaven's unfolding story. Joy anchors you when pressure builds. Joy keeps you steady when the launchpad trembles. Joy gives you strength to endure the final stretch of preparation. Joy reminds you that the One who holds the bow is faithful, wise, and intentional.

Being on God's launchpad also means understanding the timing of Heaven. When everything around you accelerates, you must resist the temptation to rush. Heaven moves quickly, but not recklessly. Acceleration without aim leads to wasted impact. That is why God brings His people into seasons of stillness before releasing movement. It is why the hush comes before the surge. It is why the pullback precedes the propelling. Heaven's timeline is consistent: God forms, then positions, then releases.

Many reading this are closer to release than they realize. You have felt the strain of pressure. You have lived in the tension of the in-between. You have endured the quiet of the holy hush. You have walked through the wilderness of preparation. You have experienced the global shaking that awakened spiritual hunger. You have sensed a divine pull on your heart that does not go away. All these signs point to one truth: you are standing at the threshold of divine acceleration.

You'll recognize when you're standing on God's launchpad by listening closely to the voice of the Holy Spirit. He will whisper encouragement where fear tries to whisper retreat. He will highlight strategic relationships, new directions and fresh opportunities. He will clarify assignments that once felt cloudy. He will illuminate areas of your life that must be surrendered. He will strengthen areas that felt weak. Your readiness will not be measured by how impressive you feel, but by how available you are.

Heaven is not looking for *perfect* arrows, Heaven is looking for *yielded* ones.

When the Archer releases you, every moment of strain, tension and waiting will make sense. You will discover that God was not withholding destiny from you; He was shaping you so destiny would not crush you. You will see that the shaking was preparation. You will realize that the pushback was positioning. You will understand that the silence was alignment.

Heaven is accelerating movement across the earth. God is releasing arrows into places that have resisted breakthrough for generations. Nations will feel the impact. Cities will shift. Families will awaken. Churches will expand. Prodigals will return. The Spirit will move with urgency and tenderness in ways that astonish even seasoned believers.

The Archer is steady.
His aim is perfect.
His timing is flawless.

The question remains before every believer reading these words:

Are you ready for what's coming?

JESUS PRACTICED PULLBACK OFTEN

When believers hear the word "pullback," they often think of struggle, tension or hardship. Yet one of the clearest examples of divine pullback happened in the life of Jesus. Before any major moment of Kingdom power, Jesus stepped into intentional withdrawal. He pulled away not because He lacked strength, but because the mission ahead required focus, clarity, and alignment with His Father. These quiet moments were not interruptions in His ministry; they were the furnace that shaped every public miracle that followed. Jesus modeled something that many in the church forget: withdrawal in God's Kingdom is preparation.

Whenever the Gospels reveal the rhythm of Jesus' life, the pattern stands undeniable. He moved into crowds, but He withdrew before influence swallowed intimacy. He stepped into miracles, but He pulled back before glory overshadowed obedience. He confronted darkness, but He stepped aside before fatigue could cloud discernment. Jesus understood the necessity of retreat long before the modern church struggled to embrace it. He knew that continual output without sacred refilling leads to spiritual erosion. So, He pulled back, again and again, teaching us that divine strength is born in stillness.

Jesus' pullback moments were not signs of weakness; they were signs of strategic wisdom. Each time He withdrew, He stepped into deeper alignment with the Father, securing the clarity needed for the work ahead. The pullback was His training ground, His communion chamber, His place of recalibration. Heaven's power flowed through Him because He consistently returned to the One who sent Him.

JESUS RETREATING FOR PRAYER, ALIGNMENT, POWER AND CLARITY

The Bible repeatedly highlights Jesus' rhythm of retreat. He slipped away early in the morning to pray. He climbed hillsides to seek His Father's voice. He stayed behind when crowds dispersed. He turned solitary spaces into sanctuaries where His heart grew still enough to hear Heaven's whisper.

These were not brief pauses. They were deliberate choices. Jesus knew His strength did not arise from talent or charisma. It came from communion. His authority flowed from alignment. His miracles flowed from connection. His wisdom flowed from intimacy. Everything He carried in public came from what He gained in private.

There is a distinct difference between running away from pressure and stepping into God's presence. Jesus did not retreat because He feared conflict. He withdrew so He could confront conflict with divine precision. He did not escape crowds because He felt overwhelmed. He stepped aside so He could serve them with the fullness of Heaven's compassion. He did not avoid responsibility. He realigned His spirit so that responsibility did not distort His purpose.

Jesus pulled back so He could live poured out without burning out.

In those pullback moments He received assignments for the day. He discerned the hearts He would meet. He recognized demonic schemes before they unfolded. He listened to the Father's leading instead of human expectation. The pullback protected Him from distraction. It centered Him on what mattered. It kept His heart attuned to Heaven rather than the applause of people.

Every time Jesus withdrew, His ministry advanced.

PULLBACK MOMENTS BEFORE MIRACLES

A close reading of the Gospels reveals something easy to overlook: withdrawal consistently preceded miracles. Jesus often stepped into some of His most extraordinary acts of power right after moments of solitude.

Before choosing the twelve apostles, men who would shape Christianity for centuries, Jesus spent the entire night alone in prayer. He pulled back to hear clearly. He stepped aside so that His selection would be guided not by preference but by the Father's perfect will.

Before multiplying fish and bread to feed thousands, Jesus withdrew to a quiet place. The crowd followed Him, unaware that the stillness He carried into that moment was the very atmosphere from which multiplication flowed. Compassion filled Him because He had just come from communion. The power to multiply was forged in the quiet.

Before walking on water, Jesus dismissed everyone and went up the mountain alone. What looked like a miracle of defying natural law was actually the result of a pullback moment that stabilized His spirit. His authority over storms came from the stillness He cultivated before stepping into the wind.

Before raising Lazarus, Jesus told His disciples He had already received instruction from the Father. That knowledge, spoken with absolute certainty, came from time spent listening, not from time spent panicking.

Even in Gethsemane, before facing the cross, Jesus pulled away to pray. The path ahead was heavier than anything any human would ever endure, yet He strengthened Himself through intimacy. His willingness to surrender - "Not My will, but Yours" - came through wrestling in solitude, not through public demonstration.

Miracles are the visible evidence of invisible preparation.

What Jesus did privately empowered what He accomplished publicly. The pullback became the birthplace of breakthrough.

PULLBACK MOMENTS BEFORE AUTHORITY CONFRONTATIONS

Jesus never confronted darkness casually. Every encounter with demonic power was deliberate, strategic, and saturated in authority. Crowds often marveled at how Jesus spoke as one possessing unmatched confidence. That confidence did not come from human training. It came from Heaven's confirmation.

Jesus stepped into authority confrontations only after securing divine clarity through withdrawal.

When He faced the man filled with a legion of demons, Jesus had already spent time aligning His spirit. He crossed a stormy sea to reach that one man, yet not a moment of panic touched Him. He walked into that confrontation with complete certainty because He had already received Heaven's perspective.

When religious leaders challenged Jesus with traps and accusations, He answered with wisdom that silenced them. That wisdom flowed from a reservoir built in solitude. Jesus did not speak reactionary words. He spoke words that came from the Father—words forged in stillness.

Before cleansing the temple, He entered Jerusalem fully aware of His assignment. His authority to overturn tables came from the conviction birthed in quiet communion. It was not a moment of emotional impulse - it was a moment of prophetic precision.

When He stood before Pilate, He did not defend Himself with anxiety or fear. His pullback moments had already secured in Him the strength needed to endure injustice without losing identity. He carried calm because He had knelt in quiet. He carried resolve because He had surrendered in private.

Authority flows from alignment, and alignment grows through pullback.

PULLBACK BEFORE DELIVERANCE AND MULTIPLICATION

Deliverance requires spiritual strength because it confronts unseen forces attempting to destroy God's people. Multiplication requires supernatural faith because it draws resource from realms beyond human limitation. Jesus moved in both realms effortlessly, but not because He was casual about them. His pullback moments gave Him capacity to stand in places where human strength falters.

Before driving out unclean spirits, Jesus often withdrew to pray. Scripture notes these patterns intentionally, revealing that deliverance flowed from the inner strength He cultivated with His Father. He did not rely on emotion or physical vigor. He relied on the spiritual authority shaped through stillness.

Before releasing abundance, whether through multiplying food, filling nets with fish, or revealing Kingdom mysteries, Jesus paused long enough to align His spirit with Heaven's generosity. Multiplication requires a heart free from striving. Striving disappears in stillness.

When Jesus told His disciples to cast their nets on the other side, He spoke with the confidence of someone who had heard directly from the Father. His ability to see what others could not see came from His time in solitary prayer. The pullback sharpened His spiritual sight, enabling Him to speak supernatural outcomes into natural environments.

The same principle applies to every believer. We long for miracles, breakthroughs, deliverance and multiplication, yet often neglect the sacred pullback that empowers them. Jesus never performed miracles disconnected from private communion. He understood the cost of public anointing and embraced the necessity of private alignment.

Modern culture equates withdrawing with quitting. Silence with insignificance. Solitude with weakness. But in God's Kingdom, withdrawing is not stepping back from purpose; it is stepping deeper into it. When modern culture refers to rest or taking a time of rest, they don't do that Jesus did. They speak of it as disengaging when in fact Jesus withdrew so He could go deeper, come back stronger and walk into and not away from the purpose of the mission He was already on.

Jesus withdrew not to escape responsibility, but to strengthen His ability to fulfill it. Withdrawal is Heaven's classroom, not Heaven's exit. It is where God tunes your hearing, strengthens your resolve, softens your heart, and fills your spirit with fresh oil.

When Jesus stepped away from crowds, He was not abandoning them. He was preparing to serve them with greater compassion, wisdom, and power. When He removed Himself from noise, it was not because He feared conflict. It was because clarity demands quiet. Noise corrupts discernment. Crowds cloud vision. The pullback protects the purity of purpose. It fine tunes accuracy and aim.

Withdrawal is where motives transform. It is where fear dissolves. It is where identity is restored. It is where courage grows. Jesus embraced withdrawal because He understood that fruit grows in hidden places long before it appears in public.

Every believer called into Kingdom assignment must learn this rhythm. Without pullback, strength becomes thin, clarity becomes foggy, and vision becomes distorted. Without pullback, you lose your footing in a world that demands constant activity. Without pullback, you fight battles you were never instructed to fight.

God calls His people into withdrawal because He wants them to rise with accuracy, not exhaustion.

To step away with God is to step toward purpose.

Jesus modeled this rhythm so we would not neglect it. He demonstrated the necessity of tending the inner life. He revealed that communion precedes calling, and intimacy precedes impact.

THE PULLBACK OF JESUS AS OUR MODEL

If Jesus, the Son of God, filled without measure by the Spirit, chose to withdraw regularly, how much more must we? If He refused to minister without receiving strength from the Father, how much more should we protect our communion? If He refused to trust His own strength apart from prayerful alignment, how much more should we guard our hearts from self-reliance?

Jesus did not withdraw because He needed rescue. He withdrew because He needed rhythm.

His life teaches us that the most powerful people in the Kingdom are not those who work constantly, but those who withdraw consistently. They do not run on adrenaline. They run on anointing. They do not react to pressure. They respond to the Father's voice. They do not crumble when crowds disappear. They stand firm because their roots run deep.

Pullback is where roots grow.

Jesus practiced pullback to teach us the difference between activity and assignment, between movement and mission, between emotional energy and spiritual authority. He revealed that power without stillness is unstable, and purpose without intimacy is unsustainable.

PULLBACK AS PREPARATION FOR WHAT'S COMING

Jesus stepped into some of the most remarkable moments in history because He trained His spirit in solitude. His pullback prepared Him for every confrontation, miracle, teaching and sacrifice ahead. He lived forward because He withdrew backward.

This is the rhythm of the Kingdom:
Pull back.
Align.
Rise.
Advance.

Jesus practiced this rhythm often so His followers could imitate it. He carried victory because He carried stillness. He carried glory because He carried surrender. He carried impact because He carried intimacy.

If Jesus lived this way, then every disciple is called into the same posture. You cannot bypass pullback and walk in the fullness of destiny. You cannot skip solitude and expect clarity. You cannot avoid alignment and expect accuracy.

Pullback is the doorway into spiritual authority.

It was for Jesus.
It is for us.

SURRENDERED TO THE ARCHER

Surrender in the Kingdom never resembles defeat. In God's hands, surrender becomes strength, stability and precision. It is the posture that allows your life to travel farther than your own effort ever could. Many believers misunderstand surrender because they imagine it strips agency or diminishes identity. Yet the opposite is true. Surrender places your entire being into the hands of Someone who knows you better than you know yourself. When the Archer holds an arrow, the arrow does not lose purpose, but its purpose becomes clearer than ever.

Yielding to God is not passivity; it is partnership. It is the decision to trust the One who sees the whole field instead of trusting your limited vantage point. It is choosing alignment over independence, direction over drift, design over self-driven motion. Every arrow finds its meaning only when it yields to the Archer. A life surrendered to God becomes extremely accurate and uncommonly precise when it comes to reaching the high goals set before it.

Surrender reveals your understanding of God's character. If He is viewed as unpredictable or harsh, surrender feels dangerous. But when your heart recognizes Him as faithful, wise, intentional and tender, surrender becomes the safest place imaginable. You do not release control into emptiness, you release it into the steady, skilled hands of the One who has guided generations. Yielding to the Archer is not a collapse; it is a deliberate choice to rest in His grip.

In natural thinking, yielding feels like losing ground. But in the Kingdom, yielding is the very act that activates strength. You cannot be propelled, guided or aimed while gripping control with clenched fists. Strength comes from trusting God with the parts of your life that refuse to bend under pressure. Surrender is courage!

God never forces surrender. Compulsion cannot create obedience that carries longevity. He invites surrender so that your spirit can hold the shape needed for future movement. Yielding prepares the heart for what power will demand. Every move of God requires believers who stand firm yet remain flexible under His command. Surrender is the training ground for that flexibility.

The world applauds self-promotion and self-preservation, but Heaven honors submission. Heaven invests authority in those who trust God enough to let Him lead them through seasons they would never choose on their own. Some of the strongest believers you will ever meet are those who appear most yielded. They walk with quiet confidence because they know the Archer is guiding every part of their story.

Yielding breaks the illusion of self-sufficiency. It teaches you that strength without surrender becomes brittle, yet strength shaped by surrender becomes unbreakable. God can aim a yielded heart far more effectively than He can aim a resistant one.

One of the most difficult aspects of surrender is allowing God to decide the direction of your life. The Archer, *not the arrow*, chooses the aim. He determines the timing of release. He picks the target. He controls the distance. The arrow simply yields to the hand that shapes its flight.

There are seasons in your life where you will not understand God's direction. His aim may seem unusual or even counterintuitive. He may angle your life toward people, places or purposes that do not look like the fulfillment you expected. He may point you toward assignments that feel too large or too hidden. He may delay release long after you feel ready. He may accelerate movement when you feel unprepared. None of this is random. His aim is perfect even when the target is not immediately visible.

The Archer's perspective is higher than yours. He sees the terrain, the wind, the obstacles, the timing of every opening. He sees where impact will matter most. He sees the ripple effect your obedience will create. He sees the exact moment when release will strike the target with maximum force.

Because His aim is flawless, surrender becomes wisdom.

There will be days when you feel God is leading you the long way round, rather than the direct path. That long way is deliberate. The Archer does not release arrows into landscapes where they cannot endure.

Then it came to pass, when Pharaoh had let the people go, that God did not lead them by way of the land of the Philistines, although

that was near; for God said, "Lest perhaps the people change their minds when they see war, and return to Egypt."
— Exodus 13:17

Sometimes it's more time on the potter's wheel we need. Is it possible for us to overestimate our readiness and underestimate our trust in God. He takes you the long way to build the internal weight needed to withstand the flight. Distance in the Kingdom requires depth. Preparation produces accuracy. What feels like detour from your perspective may be protection from His.

Once you grasp that God's aim is intentional, surrender no longer feels like loss. It feels like relief.

TRUST STRETCHED THROUGH DISCOMFORT

True trust grows only when tested. It expands through seasons when circumstances do not match expectations. Discomfort becomes the stretching ground of faith, not its destruction. God allows these tension-filled spaces because they expose what your heart clings to when everything familiar begins to shift.

Trust is not developed in ease. It grows in uncertainty. It grows in the moments where you do not see the answer, yet you believe the Archer has not loosened His grip. It grows in the nights where your prayers echo through silence, yet you cling to His character. It grows in the trials when your strength reaches its end, yet grace meets you there.

Discomfort reveals your anchor points. If your anchor rests in results, surrender will always feel unstable. If your anchor rests in God's nature, surrender becomes steady regardless of circumstances.

The stretching of trust is not punishment. It is God strengthening your foundation for what comes next. When He releases you, the winds you face will require a trust that cannot be easily shaken. Discomfort builds that trust. It deepens your reliance on the Archer's guidance. It teaches you to rest in His decisions rather than your own.

Many believers mistake discomfort for divine displeasure. Yet discomfort often signals that God is shaping parts of your character that would limit your distance if left unaddressed. The Archer does not stretch you to break you. He stretches you to strengthen you.

HEARTS SHAPED LIKE ARROWS: SANDED, STRAIGHTENED, BALANCED AND POLISHED

In the ancient world, arrows did not begin as smooth, symmetrical tools of precision. They began as rough branches, crooked, uneven and full of imperfections. An archer would choose a piece of wood not because it was perfect, but because he saw what it could become. He would sand it to remove splinters. He would straighten it through heat and pressure. He would balance it by adjusting weight distribution. He would polish it until friction could no longer disrupt flight.

This process was not gentle. Sanding scraped. Straightening heated. Balancing required cutting. Polishing demanded repetition. Yet every moment of shaping carried purpose. When the arrow finally rested in the Archer's hand, it flew true because it had submitted to the shaping.

Your heart undergoes a similar process under God's care. He sands away the parts that snag your calling. He straightens what has grown bent through disappointment or pride. He balances areas that feel heavy or underdeveloped. He polishes your character so the winds of transition cannot throw you off course.

You are not shaped by accident; you are shaped with intention.

Every trial you endured became part of the sanding. Every correction He gave became part of the straightening. Every delay became part of the balancing. Every moment in His presence became part of the polishing.

No arrow resents its formation once it discovers how true its flight becomes. What felt harsh in the moment becomes honor in hindsight. God's shaping is evidence that He sees destiny in you worth preparing for.

When Israel left Egypt, God did not take them along the shortest route to the promised land. God's Word notes that He deliberately led them by the longer way, protecting them from battles they were not ready to face. It was not indecisiveness on God's part. It was not punishment. The long way built identity, discipline, unity and trust.

God still leads His people through the long way at times because the short way would destroy unprepared hearts. He uses extended seasons of development to anchor convictions that cannot be shaken by pressure or influence. Conviction formed quickly, crumbles quickly. Conviction formed in the long way becomes unbreakable.

The long way teaches perseverance. It reveals what your heart values. It uncovers misplaced confidence. It strengthens your endurance. It refines your motives. It builds the spiritual architecture required to hold the weight of your future.

Some of the longest seasons of your life have not been wasted. They have been protective barriers! God saw battles on the short route you did not see. He saw traps that would have ensnared you. He saw temptations that would have derailed you. He saw relationships that would have wounded you. He took you the long way so you could arrive whole, healed and mature.

The long way also stabilizes purpose. When God takes His time with you, He anchors your convictions in truth rather than emotion. Purpose forged in emotion collapses when the environmental winds shift. Purpose forged in conviction withstands storms.

If the Archer prepares you longer than you expected, it is because the flight He has designed for you requires greater resilience than you yet possess. The long way is an investment.

SURRENDER AS THE HIGHEST FORM OF READINESS

Surrender positions you for release. It readies your heart to follow God without requiring full explanation. It places your life into the flow of His wisdom rather than the weight of your own understanding. The Archer does not release arrows that resist His aim. He releases arrows that trust His hand.

Surrender allows God to redirect you without resistance, to correct you without defensiveness, to refine you without resentment. It transforms obedience from obligation into joy. It removes pressure from your shoulders and places it on His. You were not designed to carry the responsibility of aim. You were designed to trust the One who aims you.

A surrendered life flies farther because it fights less.

When you yield to the Archer, momentum comes naturally. Doors open at the correct time. Strength rises when needed. Courage becomes a consistent companion. Wisdom flows without striving. You do not have to determine every outcome, you simply follow His lead.

The greatest victories in the Kingdom are accomplished by those who surrender long before they are released. Victory begins in the yielding.

Your part is not to control the bow.
Your part is not to predict the moment.
Your part is not to choose the target.
Your part is not to manage the wind.

Your part is to surrender.

When the Archer sees a heart fully yielded, He knows the arrow is ready.

CHAPTER 8

DON'T WIND UP IF YOU'RE NOT WILLING TO LET GO

———————

Every move of God in your life travels through a pattern: pullback, wind-up, release.

The pullback forms strength. The wind-up creates tension and focus. The release carries you into destiny. Most believers eagerly embrace the wind-up season because they sense movement building beneath the surface. They feel the tension, the anticipation, the internal readiness. They notice doors shifting, atmospheres changing, thoughts sharpening. Everything feels like it is leading toward something greater. And it is. But the wind-up has a purpose that many forget: it prepares you for letting go.

You cannot ask God to wind you up and then refuse release. The Archer does not generate tension for nothing. He draws the bowstring back so the arrow can fly. Without release, the wind-up becomes wasted energy. Many believers want momentum without surrender. They want acceleration while keeping control. They crave spiritual velocity while gripping the familiar. But an arrow cannot carry authority if it refuses to leave the Archer's hand.

Letting go is one of the most difficult acts of faith because it demands trust in the unseen. You must let go before you see the target. You must let go before you feel the wind beneath you. You must let go before results appear. The wind-up season builds the inner capacity needed to make that moment possible. God stretches your faith until release becomes obedience rather than fear.

The contradiction many believers carry, longing for momentum while resisting surrender, creates internal conflict. You cannot fly while anchored to control. You cannot move forward while gripping outcomes. You cannot step into destiny while negotiating with God over details He has already planned. The wind-up reveals whether your trust rests in God's aim or your own understanding.

THE CONTRADICTION OF WANTING MOMENTUM WITHOUT SURRENDER

Momentum requires relinquishing the right to manage the journey. God does not create supernatural movement merely to enhance your comfort. He creates movement because He has something for you to reach, someone for you to impact, territory for you to occupy, and purposes woven into eternity that need your obedience. When a believer cries out for momentum, Heaven listens, but Heaven also responds with a question: *"Are you prepared to release control?"*

The contradiction emerges when a believer wants God to move mountains but refuses to move their grip. They want divine acceleration without divine authority. They want the speed of Heaven with the security of self-direction. Yet Kingdom momentum is not mechanical. It is relational. It flows through trust, not technique.

The wind-up season exposes this contradiction. As tension builds, you begin to realize you cannot maintain both control and obedience. The more God prepares you, the more obvious it becomes that release is the only pathway forward. Tension is wasted unless the arrow flies. Faith collapses unless it surrenders. Destiny remains dormant unless you yield.

Contrary to how you normally picture it, momentum is not created by motion, it is created by release.

THE DANGER OF CLINGING TO CONTROL IN A SEASON MEANT FOR RELEASE

Clinging to control is dangerous because it distorts your posture. When you attempt to dictate direction, timing, and outcome, you tug against the Archer's hand. That resistance can bend the arrow, weaken its strength, and disrupt its trajectory. The enemy does not need to stop your launch; he only needs to convince you to hold on too tightly.

Control feels safe, especially when past disappointments have shaped your expectations. Many believers cling to control because they fear repeating past mistakes or revisiting past pain. Control becomes a self-made shield against vulnerability. But control cannot protect you in the spiritual realm, only surrender can. Control blocks destiny because it prevents movement. Control interrupts purpose because it keeps you rooted in fear.

A season meant for release becomes a season of stagnation when control dominates your decisions. God may have prepared everything around you for breakthrough—relationships, opportunities, spiritual maturity, doors of influence—yet nothing moves until you let go. The wind-up loses meaning when the arrow resists release.

Control also creates false targets. When you cling to your own vision of success, you aim your life at places God never intended. These false targets may look attractive, secure or logical, but they fall short of divine purpose. You may convince yourself they are close enough. But close enough is not obedience. Close enough is not the high call of God. Close enough is compromise wrapped in convenience.

The Archer aims with perfect accuracy. You aim with limited perspective. The danger of control is simple: it replaces divine precision with human estimation.

Letting Go of Outcomes

Letting go begins with releasing your need to manage outcomes. Many believers hesitate to surrender because they fear what letting go might cost. They worry that obedience will lead them into loss, disappointment or uncertainty.

But obedience leads you into promise. Outcomes belong to God. Obedience belongs to you.

Letting go of outcomes means trusting that God sees the full field. He knows where the arrow will hit. He knows the ripple effect that impact will have. When you hold outcomes too tightly, you carry weight never meant for your shoulders. You become exhausted managing what only God can control.

Letting go of outcomes means elevating trust.

Letting Go of Fear

Fear is the strongest form of internal resistance to release. Fear whispers that the arrow is safer in the Archer's hand. Fear insists that movement is dangerous. Fear magnifies uncertainty until obedience feels reckless. But fear cannot coexist with faith. And fear cannot dictate decisions in the Kingdom.

Fear is a false prophet. It predicts outcomes that God never intended. It exaggerates risks and downplays the presence of God. It shapes your imagination into a worst-case battlefield. When you cling to fear, you treat the wind-up as threat instead of preparation.

Faith dismantles fear not by denying reality, but by anchoring you in God's character. Faith remembers that the Archer is good. Faith believes that the release will not destroy you. Faith trusts that the winds ahead carry purpose, not peril.

Letting go of fear does not happen in a single moment. It happens through repeated choices to trust God over your emotions. As trust grows, fear loses its authority.

Letting Go of Timelines

God's timing rarely aligns with human timelines. He moves at the pace that protects your heart and maximizes purpose. But many believers hold tightly to personal timelines: deadlines for breakthrough, expectations for growth, and imagined milestones for success. These timelines create pressure God never assigned.

The wind-up season is the time when God dismantles your timelines. He reveals that speed without surrender creates disaster. He reveals that movement without timing creates misalignment. He reveals that His timing is not slow, it is sovereign.

Letting go of timelines frees your spirit from unnecessary anxiety. It invites you into trust rather than striving. It removes the urgency to force outcomes and enables you to recognize divine moments when they arrive.

When you release your timeline, you discover that God's timing is always better than your prediction.

Letting Go of Past Disappointments

Disappointment is one of the heaviest weights a believer can carry into a wind-up season. Past pain creates internal hesitation. Past betrayals create emotional caution. Past failures create mental resistance. These experiences shape expectations and often cause believers to grip control more tightly.

But disappointment cannot be allowed to define your direction. Every arrow must live in the future! You are not being released toward your past; you are being released toward your future. You cannot fly if you are anchored to wounds that God has already healed or wants to heal.

Letting go of disappointment means acknowledging pain without allowing it to lead you. It means recognizing that God is not recycling old seasons, He is creating new ones. It means forgiving what needs forgiveness and releasing what needs release.

Letting Go of False Targets

A false target is any aim that looks right but does not align with God's assignment. False targets can be created through ambition, comparison, insecurity, or cultural pressure. They promise impact but lack divine sanction. They offer recognition but steal purpose.

Many believers wind up spiritually and then aim at the wrong target because they never surrendered direction. They confuse opportunity with calling. They confuse applause with fruitfulness. They confuse busyness with obedience.

God does not ask you to hit every target—only the one He chooses.

Letting go of false targets requires spiritual maturity. It requires humility to say, "Lord, not my aim, but Yours." It requires the courage to walk away from attractive paths that God never designed for you. It requires discernment to recognize when something good is not something God.

You cannot hit the right target if your heart is clinging to the wrong one.

FAITH AS THE RELEASE MECHANISM

In the Kingdom, faith is the mechanism that initiates release. God can pull you back. He can position you. He can strengthen you. He can aim you with perfect accuracy. But the actual moment of launch requires a response from your spirit. When the Archer opens His hand, the arrow must trust the flight.

Faith is not emotion. Faith is agreement. It is the act of aligning your heart with what Heaven has declared. It is the decision to step into movement that does not yet feel safe. It is the willingness to fly even when the wind is untested.

Faith transforms the wind-up into momentum. Faith lifts you above circumstance. Faith gives you permission to leave the familiar. Faith declares that the God who pulled you back knows how to carry you forward.

Faith is the moment you say, "Lord, I let go."

The release requires trust. When your heart releases, movement follows. When movement follows, impact becomes inevitable.

This is why God builds faith before release. Faith is the only posture that allows you to fly without fear, rise without hesitation, and land exactly where Heaven intends.

Letting go is a series of decisions. You let go of control today, then again tomorrow, then again next week. You release fear in the morning and refuse to reclaim it at night. You surrender outcomes repeatedly until surrender becomes your natural posture. You choose obedience over security again and again.

The Spirit is calling believers in this hour to release their grip. Heaven is preparing to launch many into prophetic assignments, Kingdom influence, supernatural expansion and fresh territories. But the wind-up has meaning only if you let go. This is the season where God asks His people to trust the tension, lean into His aim, and embrace the moment of release without fear.

You cannot wind up without willingness to fly.
You cannot be positioned without willingness to move.
You cannot be refined without willingness to surrender.
You cannot be aimed without willingness to trust.

God has prepared you.
God has strengthened you.
God has positioned you.
Now He is asking, will you let go?

PART III: PRAYER, AIM, RESET, FIRE

CHAPTER 9

PRAYERS THAT BREAK THROUGH

Prayer has never been a passive spiritual discipline. It is not the quiet corner of faith where words drift upward without consequence. Prayer is not a pause, not a delay, not a spiritual holding pattern. Prayer is an intentional moment when God draws your spirit into alignment so He can release you into breakthrough. Every great movement of God in Scripture and history began not with human strategy, but with the unseen pullback of prayer. When believers kneel, Heaven tightens the bowstring. When believers cry out, Heaven draws them into readiness. When believers intercede, Heaven aims them.

Prayer is the most powerful form of divine tension you will ever encounter. It stretches your spirit toward faith. It presses your heart toward surrender. It awakens your vision. Prayer sharpens. Prayer cleanses. Prayer reorients your sight toward the target God has chosen. Many see prayer as a break in momentum, but

Heaven sees it as the mechanism that *creates* momentum. Prayer empowers action.

When you pray, you step into the pullback chamber of Heaven, where purpose is clarified, strength is formed, and boldness is born.

Too often believers treat prayer as the last resort, the thing you turn to when strategy fails or when a problem grows too large to manage. But prayer was never meant to be a spiritual bandage. It is the bowstring in God's hand. When the Spirit draws you into prayer, He is not removing you from the battlefield; He is preparing you to re-enter it with supernatural accuracy.

Prayer is the pullback that restores alignment.

Prayer is the pullback that clears confusion.

Prayer is the pullback that forms courage.

Prayer is the pullback that heals hidden wounds.

Prayer is the pullback that convinces your heart that God is still leading, still aiming, still working.

When believers understand prayer this way, everything shifts. Instead of feeling stalled, they feel strengthened. Instead of feeling sidelined, they feel refined. Instead of wondering why the "action" has slowed, they begin seeing that their greatest breakthroughs are waiting in the unseen tension of intercession.

The enemy knows the pullback of prayer is dangerous to his plans. That is why he fights prayer more than any other practice. But every time he tries to silence your voice, he forgets one truth: an arrow pulled back will always travel farther than an arrow released too soon.

Prayer is Heaven's strategic delay. Not a delay that frustrates, but a delay that fortifies.

The deepest prayers often rise not from comfort but from pressure. Pressed-down seasons create prayer that carries weight. Pressed-down places birth warriors instead of observers. Pressed-down moments carve space in the heart that normal circumstances never would have opened.

These pressed-down prayer places are where God increases capacity. When life compresses you, it pushes unnecessary clutter from your spirit. Pressure clarifies what matters and what does not. It strips away self-reliance, dismantles pride, exposes unhealthy attachments, and awakens desperate hunger for God's presence.

And in that desperation, accuracy is formed.

When the heart is stripped of distractions, prayers become sharper. When the soul is pressed to its limits, prayers become honest. When disappointment shouts, your voice begins to cry out with authenticity. Heaven listens with great attention when prayer rises from places where nothing else makes sense but God.

Accuracy in prayer does not come from fancy language. It comes from purity. It comes from letting God press you into deeper places, so your prayer carries depth instead of noise. What you see as pressure, Heaven sees as preparation. What you call heaviness, Heaven calls sharpening.

The Spirit uses these pressed-down moments to stretch your spiritual lungs. You learn to breathe deeper in God's presence. You learn to hold faith longer. You learn to carry intercession with strength instead of fragility. Pressed-down prayer produces fire instead of fear.

NICO SMIT

INTERCESSION AS WINDUP FOR SUPERNATURAL MOVEMENT

Before arrows fly, they feel the tight pull of wind-up. Before breakthroughs manifest, the saints feel the inner stirring of intercession. The two are identical in nature. Intercession is the wind-up that precedes divine release.

Intercession gathers the spiritual tension needed for movement. It builds momentum in the unseen realm long before results appear in the natural. When you intercede, you join the tug of Heaven against the resistance of darkness. You step into the stretch between promise and manifestation. That stretch is sacred. It is where Heaven shapes strength.

Intercession is not quiet. It may appear silent externally, but spiritually it is thunder. It shakes foundations. It confronts the enemy. It summons angelic activity. It awakens dormant promises. It summons breakthrough in realms human eyes cannot see.

Many believers underestimate intercession because it doesn't produce instant results. But intercession is not microwaved prayer—it is the deep pottery wheel of God. It forms endurance, shape, and weight within your spirit. It positions you for sudden movement.

There are divine wind-up moments where pressure builds just before release. Intercession mirrors that dynamic perfectly. Prayer creates spiritual torque. When God says "now," the combined momentum of your intercession and His sovereign timing sends you forward with force no demon can hinder.

Intercession is spiritual engineering. It constructs the runway for miracles. It opens passageways no human effort could unlock.

It grabs hold of God's promises and refuses to let go. It joins Heaven's aim with earth's agreement.

Every move of God begins in intercession. Every revival births in secret places before it floods public places. Every prophetic arrow moves because someone prayed with tenacity. Intercession prepares the atmosphere for God to move. It winds up Heaven's assignment. It declares, "Lord, release what You've positioned."

PRAYERS THAT AIM: BOLD, FOCUSED, RELENTLESS, FAITH-DRIVEN

The prayers that shift atmospheres are not timid. They are not hesitant. They are not vague. They are prayers that aim.

When Heaven looks for believers who will pray breakthrough prayers, God is not looking for poetic language. He looks for hearts that believe Him without wavering. Bold prayers flow from bold faith. Focused prayers flow from clear alignment. Relentless prayers flow from deep conviction. Faith-driven prayers flow from absolute trust in what God has spoken.

Bold prayer refuses to shrink back when circumstances resist. It speaks God's promises louder than fear. It dares to pray for outcomes that stretch human imagination. It stands on Scripture with confidence. Bold prayer declares Heaven's intention even when earth looks barren.

Focused prayer aims directly at God's chosen target. It does not scatter energy across a hundred different directions. It asks, "Lord, what are You pointing me to?" Then it prays with precision. Focused prayer is sharp, disciplined and intentional. Heaven responds to focused prayer because focus signals readiness.

Relentless prayer refuses to quit. It wrestles like Jacob until breakthrough arrives. It presses like Elijah until the cloud forms. It contends like Hannah until the womb opens. Relentless prayer does not surrender simply because the answer delays.

Faith-driven prayer speaks in agreement with Heaven even when the natural contradicts it. It prays as though the answer has already formed. It prays from victory, not toward it. It prays with the authority of someone who knows the Archer has aimed them.

Breakthrough prayer combines all four: boldness, focus, relentlessness and faith. When these converge, prayer transforms from a discipline into a force.

PRAYER THAT SHIFTED EVERYTHING

Ziklag was a defining moment of divine reversal. Few stories capture the essence of breakthrough prayer like David's crisis there. Ziklag was a place of ashes, loss, betrayal and despair. Everything David valued had been taken. His men, grief-stricken and furious, considered turning against him. Strength had drained from every heart.

But in that darkest moment, Scripture reveals a phrase loaded with power:
"David encouraged himself in the Lord."

This was not positive thinking. It was prayer. It was the cry of a warrior refusing defeat. It was the pullback that preceded an historic comeback.

David stepped away into intercession. He sought the Lord. He asked for direction. He poured out his anguish. He aligned his heart with God's promise. In that pullback moment, David found clarity, and Heaven answered.

God told him, "Pursue. Overtake. Recover all."

Prayer turned ashes into fuel. Prayer turned confusion into strategy. Prayer turned sorrow into strength. Prayer turned retreat into pursuit. Ziklag shifted because David prayed. Without that prayer, history would have told a different story.

Ziklag teaches this:
Breakthrough does not begin when circumstances change.
Breakthrough begins the moment your heart turns upward.

David prayed, and Heaven pulled the bowstring to its fullest tension. When God released him, he struck with precision, recovered everything and stepped into his next season of destiny.

Ziklag prayer alters everything because it is prayer born from desperation, humility and unshakeable trust.

PRAYER THAT BREAKS BARRIERS AND OPENS GATES

Breakthrough prayer is not gentle. It is fierce. It confronts demonic resistance. It dismantles spiritual blockades. It lifts heaviness from regions. It destroys lies. It releases angelic assistance. It pulls future promise into present reality.

When believers engage in barrier-breaking prayer, they become arrows of intercession. Their words carry spiritual momentum. Their petitions release Kingdom fire into the unseen realm. Their prayers shift atmospheres. Heaven moves because prayer refuses to let earth remain unchanged.

Barrier-breaking prayer does not stop when change is slow. It keeps striking. It keeps pressing. It keeps believing. It keeps aiming. It keeps releasing.

Heaven responds to persistence because persistence proves you believe God's character above your circumstances.

THE ARCHER PARTNERS WITH PRAYER

There is a mystery woven throughout God's Word: God chooses to release many of His purposes in partnership with prayer. He does not pull back the bowstring merely to impress the heavens. He pulls it back because someone on earth is praying, aligning, contending and agreeing with Him.

This is why surrender matters. This is why intercession matters. This is why bold, focused prayers matter. Prayer is the trigger of Kingdom movement. The Archer draws the bow, but prayer gives consent for release.

When you pray, you step into divine collaboration. You say, "Lord, what You are aiming me toward, I agree with. What You desire to do, I welcome. What You have spoken, I declare. What You have promised, I expect."

Prayer becomes the convergence of God's aim and your agreement.

Every answered prayer begins before the answer appears. Breakthrough always births in the invisible long before it manifests in the visible. Just as seeds break underground before they break through soil, prayers crack open spiritual ground before physical change arrives.

The invisible realm reacts immediately when faith-filled prayers rise. Angels receive assignments. Darkness retreats. Atmospheres shift. Chain reactions begin. God's Word, prayed with conviction, becomes a spiritual arrow that pierces through resistance.

Breakthrough does not start the day you see change. Breakthrough starts the moment you pray in alignment with Heaven.

THIS IS THE HOUR FOR BREAKTHROUGH PRAYER

We are living in a time where the Spirit is stirring believers to pray beyond convenience. God is calling His people to pray with fire, focus and faith. Not with passivity, but with prophetic conviction. Not with resignation, but with expectation. Not with hesitation, but with alignment.

This is the hour for prayers that pull back Heaven's bowstring.
This is the hour for intercession that winds up Kingdom movement.
This is the hour for believers who pray until the earth feels the impact.

This is the hour for Ziklag prayer - prayer that refuses despair, seeks God's direction, and pursues recovery with Heaven's authority. Breakthrough is already being set in motion through your prayers!

A RESET IS A RE-AIM WITH PURPOSE

Every significant move of God includes a moment where He places His hand upon your life and shifts your direction. Not because you failed and not because you wandered off course, but because the next season requires a new trajectory. Heaven's resets are not random interruptions; they are intentional re-aiming movements that re-align your life into the exact position needed for the assignment ahead. When God resets you, He is refining your aim.

A divine reset does something that human planning cannot accomplish. It clears away the noise, breaks old patterns, releases you from expired seasons, and positions you for impact you did not see coming. Resets are moments of spiritual recalibration. God resets to protect you. God resets to sharpen you. God resets to reposition you for weightier purpose than you carried before.

This theme appears over and over: God invites His people to review, repent, refocus.

This is compassion. Heaven is saying, "Come back into alignment. Let Me aim you again. Let Me show you the target I have prepared."

Every believer encounters these reset moments. Some come quietly. Some come through disruption. Some appear as divine interruptions that stop you midstride. Some arrive wrapped in disappointment. Others come through unexpected opportunity. But behind each reset stands the Archer who refuses to let your life drift from His sight.

A reset is Heaven saying:
"I have something ahead of you that requires a clearer aim."

God's resets are always purposeful. When He touches your direction, He adjusts not only where you are headed but how you are headed there. He refines posture, corrects angle, purifies motive, strengthens resolve, and widens perspective.

The Archer never pulls back, winds up, and releases without intention. He sees the invisible. He sees further than you can. He sees the obstacles you cannot yet discern, the opportunities you cannot yet perceive, and the timing you cannot yet calculate. Heavenly resets ensure your trajectory matches His vision instead of your limited understanding.

A reset may feel like the end of something, but Heaven sees it as the beginning of something that requires greater accuracy. God does not waste motion. Every adjustment serves purpose. Every correction builds capacity. Every re-aim prepares you for a flight that demands precision.

Sometimes God resets because your life has subtly drifted...an inch here, a distraction there, a compromise that felt small, a habit that slowly warped your focus. You do not always notice the drift, but He does. And His reset puts your sight back where it belongs.

Sometimes God resets because the assignment ahead requires new skills, new relationships, new thinking, new courage, new holiness. The direction He once used for your growth may not be the direction He uses for your impact.

Sometimes God resets because what you prayed for is now ready to arrive. And you cannot enter the promise with the posture of the last season.

Reset is God's way of ensuring that the outcome aligns with His original intention.

REVIEW, REPENT, REFOCUS — HEAVEN'S RESET PATTERN

There is a prophetic pattern: Review, Repent, Refocus - this pattern mirrors Scripture's design for divine course correction.

1. Review

Review is Heaven's invitation to look honestly at where you've been. Not with shame, but with clarity. Review examines your steps, your patterns, your choices, your priorities. Review opens the heart before God and asks, "Lord, show me where my aim drifted." It is the spiritual pause that reveals hidden motives and neglected areas. Review is illumination.

When the Spirit calls for review, He is not exposing you to condemn you. He is exposing you to heal you, to strengthen you, to realign you. Review shows you which weights you must drop, which distractions you must remove, which relationships require adjustment, which habits no longer serve purpose.

2. Repent

Clean the scope you look through. Repentance begins with surrender. It turns the heart back into alignment, resetting what has drifted and refocusing what has grown dull. It invites a continual cleansing of the lens through which we see, so that smudges, specks, and distortions no longer shape our direction. Repentance clears away the clutter that clouds discernment. It closes the door on wandering, interrupts the cycle of self-direction, and creates room for the Archer to take full control. Repentance whispers, *"Lord, I release my way for Yours. Take the aim again."* When repentance is present, spiritual precision returns. Without it, every reset falls short of its intended mark.

Repentance is not a sign of spiritual immaturity. It is a sign of spiritual responsiveness. Those who repent quickly grow deeply. Those who resist repentance carry the weight of misalignment far longer than necessary.

3. Refocus

Refocus is the moment Heaven turns your face toward the target. After review clears the heart and repentance clears the path, refocus sets your sight on what Heaven is pointing toward. Refocus aligns priorities. It awakens attention. It sharpens obedience. It removes the haze of past seasons.

Refocus is consecration. It means you direct your full attention to what God is doing now, not what life looked like before. It means you let the Spirit highlight what matters most in this season, so your energy, faith and obedience follow His aim rather than your habits.

Review looks back.
Repentance turns.
Refocus looks forward.

This is Heaven's reset cycle and it's simple, powerful, and transformative.

FROM PAST-MINDED TO FUTURE-AIMED

One of the greatest transformations God brings through a reset is shifting your focus from the past to the future. The human heart often clings to what is familiar because familiarity feels safe. Even unhealthy familiarity feels comforting when uncertainty looms. But you cannot hit a future target while staring backward.

Resets break the gravitational pull of the past.

Some believers remain anchored to past victories. They replay what God *used* to do, forgetting He wants to do something new. Past victories become prisons when you idolize the memory and stop expecting more.

Others remain anchored to past failures. They live under shame, regret or fear of repeating mistakes. These weights distort confidence and blur vision. Reset wipes the slate clean and lifts your eyes toward promise.

Some remain anchored to past identity; roles, assignments, titles, seasons God used temporarily but never meant to define you permanently. Reset frees you from identities that cannot travel with you into your future.

God resets you so you no longer live past-minded. He resets you so you become future-aimed: alert to what Heaven has prepared, sensitive to new instructions, open to divine opportunities, willing to embrace growth, and eager to partner with God's unfolding narrative.

The future belongs to those willing to release the past.
Reset is the bridge between the two.

WHY MANY FEEL DISORIENTED RIGHT BEFORE CLARITY ARRIVES

The moments leading up to divine clarity often feel confusing. You sense movement, but you cannot identify direction. You feel the Spirit stirring, but the specifics remain hidden. You know change is happening, but you cannot articulate what is shifting. This disorientation is the prelude to clarity.

Before the Archer releases an arrow, there is a fraction of a moment where the arrow feels tension without motion. Everything goes quiet, but everything is loaded. That final stretch is disorienting. You do not yet see the flight path. You only feel the pressure of being positioned.

Heaven often allows disorientation for several reasons:

1. Disorientation removes old reference points

When the familiar becomes unstable, you stop relying on old patterns. You begin looking for God's voice again instead of leaning on routine. Disorientation is a spiritual detox, clearing out noise so clarity can emerge.

2. Disorientation creates spiritual dependence

In unclear seasons, you do not trust your own understanding, you lean on God's. This dependence is necessary so that when clarity arrives, it arrives with humility, not arrogance.

3. Disorientation breaks internal idols

Anything you rely on more than God becomes unstable in reset seasons. Disorientation reveals where you placed confidence in systems, relationships, titles or routines instead of the One aiming your life.

4. Disorientation precedes upgraded vision

Before God reveals the new, He clears the old. You cannot perceive fresh direction while clinging to outdated expectations. Disorientation is the moment Heaven wipes the vision board clean.

5. Disorientation signals that clarity is close

Right before direction becomes unmistakable, the soul feels unsettled. It is the spiritual equivalent of stepping into a new atmosphere; you sense change before you see it.

Believers worldwide have felt "pushback" and "pullback," sensing they were being wound up for a purpose they cannot yet see. That sense of uncertainty is often the indicator that the Archer's aim has shifted and clarity is moments away.

When God resets your direction, He often resets your authority. You step into new spheres of influence, new relationships, new opportunities, new anointing. Reset seasons birth the kind of spiritual weight that cannot be fabricated through effort. Reset enlarges spiritual reach. Reset expands your capacity to carry responsibility without breaking under pressure.

Every major promotion in Scripture began with a divine reset—Abraham leaving his homeland, Joseph stepping into the palace, Moses returning to Egypt, David rising after Ziklag, Esther entering the palace at the perfect moment, Peter becoming a shepherd rather than a fisherman, Paul turning from persecutor to apostle.

Oftentimes a reset can make us feel as if we're losing something, but we must remember that reset is an upgrade!

WHAT RESET REQUIRES FROM YOU

A divine reset demands two responses: willingness and obedience.

Willingness means you stop clinging to the past and open your heart to the new. It means you stop resisting God's redirection. It means you trust Him even when the map is blank. Willingness is surrender with expectancy.

Obedience means you follow the new direction even when it challenges comfort. Obedience means you let God break old rhythms. Obedience means you let the Archer aim you without negotiation. Obedience is surrender with movement.

Reset without willingness becomes delay.
Reset without obedience becomes stagnation.
Reset with both becomes destiny.

When God resets your life, He does it for one ultimate purpose - to re-aim you so He can release you. Reset is not the final stage; it is the stage that prepares you for acceleration. It aligns posture, sharpens vision, and prepares the heart for the moment Heaven opens the Archer's fingers.

Reset refines direction.
Re-aim refines purpose.
Release refines impact.

You cannot walk into release if you resist re-aim.
You cannot embrace re-aim if you reject reset.

Reset is the invitation into the next chapter Heaven has already written.

AIMED & READY

Across the world right now, countless believers feel the shift. They feel the reset. They feel God turning their hearts toward the unseen. They feel past seasons closing. They feel new doors pulling their spirit forward. They feel the Archer adjusting aim. They feel the quiet intensity of divine reorientation.

They feel the reset.
They feel the re-aim.
They feel the coming release.

What seemed confusing is becoming strategic.
What seemed heavy is becoming holy.
What seemed destabilizing is becoming the foundation for a new launch.

God resets because He finishes what He starts.
And He resets because He knows exactly how far He intends to send you.

You are being reset with purpose.
You are being re-aimed with precision.
You are being prepared for impact.

Reset is not the end but rather the beginning of your re-aim.

STAY AIMED: LOCKED ON TARGET UNTIL YOU'RE FIRED

There comes a moment in every believer's journey when the Archer has finished shaping, sanding and straightening, the pullback has been completed, the tension has settled into place, and the aim has been fixed with surgical focus.

Nothing remains except stillness. This moment, when the arrow rests motionless yet fully charged with purpose, is one of the most sacred spaces in the Kingdom. It is here, in this poised silence, that the call is simple but weighty: **stay aimed.** Do not shift. Do not look away. Do not yield to distraction. Remain locked on the target He has chosen until the Archer releases you into the fullness of your assignment.

Many believers feel uncomfortable in this stillness because everything in human nature wants to move, to adjust, to overthink, or to second-guess what God is aiming at. Yet this is the very interval that determines accuracy. This is the moment when faith becomes focus.

Staying aimed is not something you do once; it is a posture you maintain deep in your spirit. It is a spiritual discipline, a consecrated gaze, a chosen focus when everything else falls away and only one target remains before you: Jesus—your aim, your mark, your anchor, your direction.

To stay aimed is to lift your eyes above storms, opinions, chaos and cultural noise, fixing them solely on the One whose hands hold your destiny.

PROPHETIC FOCUS

If then you were raised with Christ, SEEK those things which are above, where Christ is, sitting at the right hand of God. SET YOUR MIND ON THINGS ABOVE, not on things on the earth.
— Colossians 3:1-4 (emphasis mine)

There is an ancient principle woven into the life of every follower of Christ: *what you fix your eyes on will shape the direction you travel.* When Peter walked on water, he did not defy nature because of his own strength; he overcame the impossible because his gaze remained locked on Jesus. The moment he shifted his attention to the winds and waves, he began to sink. His failure was not due to a lack of calling but rather a loss of focus.

Focus carries spiritual authority.

When your eyes rest on Jesus, storms lose their power to intimidate. When your mind stays anchored in His word, fear loses its leverage. When your heart remains attentive to His presence, distractions dissolve.

Prophetic focus is not mystical; it is intentional. It is the consistent choice to look where Heaven is pointing rather than where circumstances are screaming.

Many believers "are drawn to the winds and waves" and miss the miracle unfolding beneath their feet. Staying aimed means your attention cannot be tossed around. You do not give storms permission to define your decisions. You do not allow the unpredictable environment to rewrite the promise God spoke. You do not let the size of the problem eclipse the size of the One pointing you forward.

Focus is your anchor.
Focus is your compass.
Focus is your protection from misalignment.

Behind you is Jesus, steady and sure. His left hand pointing to the mark, the target, the goal, the upward call and with His right hand He pulls back the arrows of your destiny. It's not a shot in the dark; it is directed by Heaven itself. When released from His hand you become an unstoppable arrow of divine purpose.

The arrow cannot turn mid-flight. The only time it can adjust is now, *before the release*, and the only adjustment Heaven asks of you is this: fix your eyes on the target God has chosen.

Avoiding Distraction

The moment you are fully aimed, distractions multiply.
Make no mistake, this is warfare. The enemy knows he cannot change the Archer's intention, so he attempts to agitate the arrow. He cannot derail God's plan, so he tries to derail your focus.

This is why staying aimed requires discernment.

Noise

Noise comes in many forms: external chatter, spiritual static, cultural pressure, internal overthinking, and more. Noise steals clarity by flooding your attention with everything except what God has said. If the enemy cannot stop you, he will attempt to drown you in irrelevant voices. Noise is not always sinful; it is simply loud. Staying aimed means silencing anything that does not align with the target.

Fear

Fear surfaces when the future demands trust. Fear whispers worst-case outcomes, magnifies uncertainty, and paints disaster across your imagination. Fear is the opposite pull of faith. But arrows do not fear the wind; they trust the Archer's release. Fear loses power when you root yourself in confidence that God did not miscalculate your trajectory.

Fatigue

Weariness blurs vision. Fatigue makes you vulnerable to doubt, impatience and compromise. Many arrows abandon their posture not because they lost calling, but because they lost strength. The holy hush is meant to restore that strength. Staying aimed includes caring for your spirit - resting, worshiping, feeding your faith - so you do not slip under the weight of the waiting.

False Narratives

These narratives are internal lies that attempt to rewrite your story:
"You missed your moment."
"You're not worthy."
"Nothing is changing."
"God isn't using you."

These lies do not come from Heaven. They come from an enemy who fears the impact of your release. Staying aimed requires refusing any narrative that contradicts God's voice.

Enemy Taunts

Just as Goliath taunted Israel to weaken their courage, the enemy taunts believers to weaken focus. Taunts are designed to provoke reaction, not obedience. But an arrow does not answer taunts; an arrow stays still. Your silence in the face of spiritual mockery becomes your strength.
To remain aimed is to guard your attention as fiercely as warriors guard their weapons. The enemy's goal is not to convince the Archer to change His aim, he knows he cannot. His goal is to convince the arrow to twist, shake or shrink back before release.

Do not give him that satisfaction!

THE APOSTOLIC RISE IN PRECISION

The church is entering a season of supernatural precision. Heaven is raising believers who carry apostolic clarity, men and women who know why they were created, where they are being sent, and who they are called to impact. This precision is the fruit of staying aimed.

Arrows represent this apostolic precision. Arrows pierce through.

The church has not been retreating but rather *winding up* for global expansion and harvest. That kind of movement requires accuracy. Heaven is not releasing random arrows. Heaven is releasing strategic ones—voices, leaders, intercessors, evangelists, prophets, innovators - each aimed at territories, industries, nations and assignments carefully chosen by God.

Precision is the new mantle resting upon the church. This is why distraction has intensified. Precision terrifies darkness. To the enemy, a scattered church is manageable. A focused church becomes unstoppable.

Those who stay aimed in this hour will carry authority that shifts regions. They will speak with clarity that cuts through confusion. They will walk with conviction that cannot be manipulated. They will move with purpose that ignites fresh faith everywhere they go.

The Archer's aim is not broad. It is exact. And He is calling you to carry that same precision.

ARROWS CANNOT FACE BACKWARD

An arrow cannot be shaped for yesterday. It cannot fly toward what is behind it. It cannot be aimed at what no longer exists. Arrows are future-bearing instruments. Their entire identity is tied to where they are going, not where they have been.

For many believers, the greatest challenge is not trusting God with the future - it is letting go of the past. Yet no arrow flies backward. No arrow replays old seasons. No arrow returns to old patterns. Once placed in the bow, the arrow faces forward and only forward.

This is why God leads His people into cycles of reset, review and re-aim. He refuses to let you live anchored to history when destiny calls from ahead. God often calls people to review, repent, refocus so they can restart with renewed clarity. That is the posture of an arrow, always oriented toward what is coming, not what has faded.

Living past-minded drains strength. Living future-minded awakens vision.

Arrows belong in tomorrow.
Arrows belong in the unfolding story of God.
Arrows belong in the fresh outpouring, the new assignment, the next move of Heaven.

When God positions you, He is not preparing you for what *was*. He is preparing you for what *will be*. Staying aimed means keeping your heart forward. Expectant. Ready. Uncluttered by history. Hungry for destiny.

The Archer does not recycle old targets. Every aim has purpose.

THE ARCHER DOES NOT MISS; STAY STEADY IN HIS GRIP

Every fear we carry in the waiting hinges on one question: *What if God misses?*
But Heaven answers that fear with unwavering truth: He does not miss. He has never missed. He cannot miss.

The Archer's accuracy is flawless.

He does not aim you toward confusion.
He does not prepare you for mediocrity.
He does not shape you for misalignment.
He does not wind you up without intention, and He does not release you by accident.

Staying steady in His grip means trusting His accuracy more than your anxieties. It means believing that His perspective is complete even when your perspective is foggy. It means understanding that His aim is perfect even when His pacing feels slow.

In the holy hush, the Archer steadies the string. In the waiting, He holds you still. In the tension, He measures distance. In the silence, He counts the cost and calculates impact.

Your job is not to determine timing—
your job is to remain steady.

Your job is not to analyze trajectory—
your job is to trust His aim.

Your job is not to predict flight conditions—
your job is to stay surrendered.

The Archer has never lost a battle. He has never misfired a promise. He has never wasted a life placed fully in His hands.

You are not the exception to His accuracy.

Stay steady. Stay aimed. Stay locked onto what He has set before you. Your release will come exactly when it must—not early, not late, and not without impact.

BREAKTHROUGH HAPPENS WHEN THE ARROW HITS THE MARK

There is a moment in every believer's journey that shifts everything. A moment when the bowstring no longer trembles with pressure. A moment when the Archer's fingers release, and the arrow that has endured shaping, sanding, waiting, silence and tension finally enters the air. That moment is breakthrough. That moment is release. That moment is the fulfillment of everything the pullback season prepared.

Breakthrough is not random. It is not luck. It is not coincidence. Breakthrough is the direct result of divine preparation. It is Heaven's answer to surrender, obedience, endurance and trust. It is evidence that the pullback was never meant to be punishment.

When God releases an arrow, the atmosphere shifts instantly. Velocity displaces the weight of waiting. Movement overtakes stillness. What dragged on for years suddenly accelerates. What resisted for months collapses in a day. What felt impossible becomes effortless. Everything that seemed dormant awakens. Everything that fought you loses strength. Everything that looked delayed transforms into divine timing.

The release is the moment Heaven says, *"Now."*

There's something I like to call the *suddenlies* of God - moments when decades of tension are swallowed up by a single divine act. These suddenlies appear often in Scripture because they reveal Heaven's rhythm. God works in patterns: long preparation, long silence, long faithfulness, and then a sudden release that changes everything in a breath.

These suddenlies redeem those painful years of waiting.

When an arrow is released, the years spent shaping no longer feel wasted. The tension does not feel cruel. The waiting does not feel meaningless. The silence does not feel punitive. Every day in the pullback finds its purpose in the moment of flight.

The suddenlies of God erase the pain of waiting not by denying it but by overwhelming it with purpose. When God moves suddenly, clarity arrives instantly. Strength rises immediately. Hope floods unexpectedly. The years that felt heavy become the foundation for impact.

Here's something important to keep in mind; A divine suddenly is perfectly timed. It only feels sudden to the one who waited.

Heaven has been preparing the release long before you sensed the shift. What looks like acceleration is actually fulfillment.

Breakthrough is when eternity touches your timeline and time surrenders to the will of God.

Things will speed up, the movements of God will intensify, the church will experience rapid growth, and what felt stagnant will suddenly ignite. This theme mirrors Scripture. When God releases someone He has prepared, advancement becomes swift.

Acceleration is Heaven's signature on a season of release.

Quick victories come where long struggles existed.
Rapid advancement replaces slow progress.
Supernatural acceleration carries you beyond your natural capability.

Why does this happen?

Because the pullback stored spiritual momentum. The tension you endured becomes thrust. The obedience you practiced becomes lift. The faith you held becomes speed. The surrender you offered becomes accuracy. The pruning you endured becomes aerodynamic power that eliminates drag.

This is why obedience matters. This is why alignment matters. This is why surrender matters. All of them build momentum that only reveals itself when release arrives.

In Scripture, whenever God released a leader into their assignment, movement followed - decisive, unstoppable and fast.

Heaven accelerates those who endured the pullback without resisting it. It is the grace to do in one year what used to take ten. It is the anointing to accomplish what once overwhelmed you. It is the supernatural push that reveals the power of God in your life.

BIBLICAL EXAMPLES TO REFLECT ON

There are numerous comeback stories throughout the Bible, moments when God transformed burial into resurrection, waiting into acceleration, setback into destiny. These stories are not historical anecdotes; they are patterns. Arrows in Scripture follow the same trajectory as arrows in your life.

Joseph
Joseph endured betrayal, slavery and false accusation. His pullback years were long, lonely and unjust. But when God released him, he rose to rulership in a single day. Acceleration erased the delay. His breakthrough revealed that every hardship carried divine intention.

Moses
Moses spent forty years in obscurity, hidden in Midian. The silence felt like erasure, but it was preparation. When God released him at the burning bush, he stepped into a calling that shook empires. His breakthrough did not reflect his wilderness it reflected God's aim.

Joshua
Joshua lived for decades as a servant, learning, watching, waiting. When his release came, he conquered territory at a pace unmatched in Israel's history. Walls fell in moments. Battles turned quickly. Movement replaced waiting.

Elijah
Elijah faced exhaustion, threats and isolation. Yet after one divine encounter, he outran Ahab's chariot - a picture of supernatural acceleration. His breakthrough showed that weariness could not steal destiny.

Peter
Peter failed publicly and bitterly. But after Jesus restored him, he preached one sermon and three thousand were saved. His release carried force his past could not diminish.

Lazarus
Lazarus's story contains the essence of divine timing. Jesus *waited* on purpose so the miracle would carry greater glory. The

pullback of delay set the stage for resurrection. The release shattered hopelessness.

Jesus

The greatest example: Jesus went through burial before breakthrough. The silence of the grave preceded resurrection power. The pullback of death became the launch of redemption.

Each story shouts the same truth:
Heaven never wastes a pullback. Heaven only uses it to release a greater breakthrough.

There is a paradox in God's ways. The hardest seasons precede the easiest breakthroughs. The deepest tension precedes the smoothest motion. This paradox confuses many believers because they expect breakthrough to feel like labor. Instead, breakthrough often feels like glide.

Why?

Because the arrow is shaped *before* it flies, not during flight.

Breakthrough is not the time of formation—breakthrough is the time of fulfillment.
Breakthrough is not the time of sanding—breakthrough is the time of soaring.
Breakthrough is not the time of tension—breakthrough is the time of impact.

The ease of breakthrough is evidence that the pullback season did its work. Here is why breakthrough feels effortless:

1. Alignment Has Already Been Achieved

Once aligned, you no longer wrestle with direction. You flow with it.

2. Resistance Has Already Been Broken

Spiritual opposition cannot restrain a released arrow. It is too late—the force is already behind you.

3. Strength Has Already Been Formed

The inner resilience built during waiting now becomes forward momentum.

4. The Archer Carries the Weight of Aim

You do not have to direct yourself. You simply allow His precision to govern the journey.

5. Breakthrough Is Fueled by Grace, Not Striving

Grace makes the flight feel light. Grace removes friction. Grace multiplies impact.

Breakthrough is the moment Heaven proves that surrender was worth it.

WHEN THE ARROW HITS THE MARK

An arrow striking its target carries sound. There is impact. There is resonance. Something shifts. Something breaks. Something opens. Something succeeds. That impact is not the result of the arrow's strength—it is the result of the Archer's aim.

When your life hits the mark God ordained:

Doors open without struggle.
Favor appears without striving.
Provision flows without manipulation.
Assignments expand without burnout.

Influence rises without self-promotion.
Testimonies multiply without forcing outcomes.

Impact is the natural expression of divine aim.

And when your arrow hits its target, breakthrough becomes contagious.
Your obedience influences others.
Your story awakens faith.
Your victory disrupts darkness in places you never saw.

Breakthrough becomes generational.
Breakthrough becomes regional.
Breakthrough becomes a testimony that echoes long after the moment passes.

Heaven releases arrows to strike targets that rewrite stories.

YOU ARE CLOSER TO BREAKTHROUGH THAN YOU THINK

Many believers are in a *divine setup*, sensing pressure not as defeat but as preparation. The bow is drawn. The tension is real. The hush is thick. And release is near.

Momentum is gathering behind you.
Clarity is forming before you.
Strength is rising within you.
Heaven is leaning toward you.

Breakthrough does not come because you forced it.
Breakthrough comes because Heaven timed it.

Everything you endured has purpose.
Everything you survived has meaning.
Everything you carried will now carry you.

When the Archer releases you, you will know it.
Nothing will hold you.
Nothing will confuse you.
Nothing will delay you.
Nothing will stop you.

The arrow flies straight.
The arrow flies strong.
The arrow flies far.
The arrow flies true.

And when the arrow hits the mark, breakthrough becomes undeniable.

PART IV: THE COMEBACK STORY

CHAPTER 13

ZIKLAG: PULLBACK BEFORE PROMOTION

Ziklag stands in Scripture as one of the most dramatic turning points in David's life. It is the place where everything seemed to collapse in a single moment - loss, betrayal, grief, exhaustion, frustration, and confusion converged into a single day that tested the core of his identity. Yet Ziklag also became the place where the deepest pullback of his life set the stage for the greatest comeback he had ever seen. What looked like devastation actually carried the seeds of promotion. What felt like abandonment became the cradle of divine acceleration. Ziklag shows us that God often allows life to draw back before He launches us forward into destiny.

When Israel finds David in 1 Samuel 30, he is not seated on a throne; he is hiding in a foreign land, living among Philistines because Saul's jealousy pushed him into exile. He is anointed but not enthroned, chosen yet still waiting, promised the crown yet chased across mountains and deserts by a king determined to destroy him. David's journey says something profound: calling does not erase struggle. In fact, calling often intensifies it. The deeper the oil, the deeper the opposition. The clearer the destiny, the more intense the pullback.

At the moment Ziklag enters the story, David has spent years running, fighting, and holding onto a promise that appears increasingly distant. Then, after returning from a mission, he finds smoke rising where his home once stood. The Amalekites raided the city, burned it to the ground, and carried off every wife, every child, every possession. The loss was total. Scripture records that David and his men wept "until they had no more strength to weep." That line captures the core of Ziklag. It is the breaking point—the moment when you have nothing left to give, no strategy left to try, no tears left to shed.

Ziklag is where strength ends but destiny begins.

LOSS THAT FEELS LIKE FINALITY

The opening act of Ziklag is devastating loss. Everything familiar has vanished in flames. Everything David once used as emotional stability has been taken. Even the loyalty of his men, his last circle of support, begins to crack. They speak of stoning him out of grief and frustration. David is alone among the ashes of everything he loves.

Loss always tries to speak a false narrative. It whispers that God has forgotten you, that promises have expired, that your leadership has failed, that breakthrough is impossible. Loss attempts to define the future based on the condition of the present. It takes the flames of Ziklag and tries to convince your heart that nothing will rise again.

Here is an important truth: believers often misread the pullback as death, when Heaven is actually preparing resurrection. Ziklag is the biblical embodiment of that revelation.

What looked like the end became the hinge that swung David into the next chapter of his calling.

Loss is not the conclusion God writes. Loss is the tension He allows before release.

STRENGTHENING YOURSELF IN THE LORD

When everything else failed, Scripture says David did something remarkable:

"But David strengthened himself in the Lord his God."

This line interrupts despair with courage. It interrupts panic with prayer. It interrupts fear with faith. Strengthening himself in the Lord was not a pep talk or a motivational pause. It was a spiritual act of recalibration. David chose to turn inward, not to collapse, but to meet God in the hidden place where identity is reaffirmed and direction is restored.

This moment mirrors the prophetic theme where believers are urged to return their focus to Jesus rather than the storm. David could not draw strength from his circumstances because they were ashes. He could not draw strength from his men because they were broken. He could not draw strength from his environment because it screamed defeat. Strength could only come from one place: God Himself.

Strengthening yourself in the Lord is refusal to let pain define destiny. It is a choice to step into God's presence when everything else pulls you toward hopelessness. It is the spiritual pullback that restores alignment before breakthrough.

Ziklag turns the moment David turns to the Lord. Breakthrough begins long before circumstances change. Breakthrough begins when the heart seeks God again.

After strengthening himself, David does the most crucial thing anyone can do during a pullback: he seeks God's instruction. He asks, "Shall I pursue? Shall I overtake?" David does not assume. He does not rush. He does not rely on past experience. He waits for the Archer's voice.

God answers with clarity, urgency and promise:
"Pursue, for you shall surely overtake them and without fail recover all."

In that moment, David receives Heaven's reset (review, repent, refocus) shifting him from grief to purpose, from paralysis to pursuit. Heaven now aims him. The target is set. Permission is given. Direction is clear. The comeback has begun.

This divine instruction carries the DNA of Heaven's re-aim. God does not simply comfort David; He commissions him. He does not soothe him with promises of sympathy; He gives him a military strategy. Ziklag teaches us that when God speaks in a season of loss, His words often push us into action rather than retreat.

God's reset is a re-aim toward future purpose - believers must tune their hearts to what He is pointing toward. David models this perfectly. He does not run blindly. He runs with divine direction.

When Heaven gives instruction, movement becomes possible again.

AIMED & READY

THE FLIGHT OF THE ARROW

Once David receives instruction, he gathers his men and pursues the Amalekites. The text describes a sequence of remarkable events: unexpected provision, divine appointments, supernatural strength, and flawless timing. Every detail aligns with Heaven's plan. They find an Egyptian servant abandoned by the enemy, who becomes the key to locating the raiders. They strike at the perfect moment when the enemy is scattered, distracted and vulnerable.

David recovers every person, every possession, every treasure. Nothing is missing. Nothing is damaged. Nothing is stolen beyond restoration. Scripture repeats the phrase "David recovered all," emphasizing that God's promise was fulfilled exactly as spoken.

This is the Ziklag pattern:
Loss → Strengthening → Instruction → Pursuit → Recovery → Promotion.

Recovery reveals the reason for the pullback. Without Ziklag, David would never have stepped into the authority that followed. Ziklag forged the warrior-king. It birthed a leader who did not crumble under pressure. It purified motives, refined vision, and prepared him for national leadership.

Many pullback seasons end with supernatural acceleration. Ziklag embodies this truth. The recovery was swift, complete and decisive. What took years to build was restored in one movement. The suddenlies of God collapsed time and replaced it with victory.

THE FINAL THRESHOLD BEFORE THE THRONE

Immediately after the Ziklag event, Saul dies in battle. The throne of Israel opens. And David, who had been running for his life, suddenly becomes king over Judah. Ziklag was the final pullback before his promotion into the very place God promised years earlier.

Promotion often follows the greatest pressure.
Elevation often follows the deepest exhaustion.
Breakthrough often follows the strongest resistance.

Ziklag was not David's failure; it was his qualifying moment. God allowed everything to burn so nothing old would cling to David when he stepped into new authority. Ziklag stripped him of the past so he could inherit the future without fragmentation. What looked like destruction was actually consecration.

Promotion in God's Kingdom is based on spiritual readiness, and Ziklag forged readiness.

Many churches and leaders entering Ziklag moments—times when everything feels shaken, stretched or broken, yet Heaven uses these moments to prepare them for expansion, harvest and global influence. Ziklag is a womb. It births destiny.

THE MOMENT GOD SAYS, "ENOUGH"

There comes a divine moment when God looks at the injustice, the suffering, the delay, the trauma, the spiritual warfare, the accusations, and the losses His people have endured and declares, "Enough." This moment shifts everything. Heaven rises. Breakthrough begins. The pullback ends.

Ziklag was that moment for David. Heaven had watched long enough. Heaven had weighed the years of exile. Heaven had measured the cost of his obedience. And Heaven determined it was time to release him into promise.

Many believers are near this moment - they are in a divine setup, positioned between the Archer's fingers, about to be launched into what they have been paying such a high price for. Ziklag represents the turning where God's "enough" becomes visible.

When God says "enough", no enemy can restrain what comes next.
When God says "enough", the tables turn.
When God says "enough", the arrow leaves the bow.
When God says "enough", recovery becomes unstoppable.

Breakthrough begins not with your strength but with God's decree.

Ziklag is a prophetic template for leaders, churches and even nations. The pattern repeats across history because the principles are universal.

1. Ziklag Strips Away Burdens That Can't Enter the New Season

Burned cities, shattered routines and uprooted systems create space for new structures, new strategies and new anointing. Churches experience this. Leaders experience this. Nations experience this. God allows shaking so that only the unshakable remains.

2. Ziklag Exposes True Strength

Pressure reveals character. Crisis reveals leadership. When everything collapses, those who strengthen themselves in the

Lord rise with authority. These are the leaders Heaven can trust with influence.

3. Ziklag Clarifies Assignment

When everything is removed, only the essential remains. Leaders rediscover vision. Churches rediscover mission. Nations rediscover purpose. Ziklag removes spiritual fog and forces clarity.

4. Ziklag Activates Divine Intervention

Heaven moves swiftly for those who refuse despair. Divine partnerships emerge. Unexpected resources appear. Miracles multiply. The comeback gains divine backing.

5. Ziklag Prepares the World for What Follows

David's kingship changed the trajectory of Israel. His reign laid foundations for the temple, the nation's expansion, and the lineage of the Messiah. Ziklag preceded global influence. Likewise, the church's global Ziklag season precedes a global revival.

Many churches are in a wind-up, preparing for worldwide expansion, and what looks like retreat is actually a divine stretch. Ziklag perfectly parallels that revelation. It is the last tightening before release.

ZIKLAG AND THE MODERN BELIEVER

Every believer faces a personal Ziklag at least once in their journey. Sometimes it appears as sudden loss, sometimes as a prolonged season of pressure, sometimes as transition that feels disorienting. But the purpose is always the same: repositioning for destiny.

If you are living through a Ziklag season, you are not at the end of your story. You are at the hinge of transformation.

AIMED & READY

Remember these crucial truths:

You are not being abandoned, you are being aimed.

You are not losing ground, you are gaining direction.

You are not being destroyed, you are being refined.

Ziklag is not where you fall.
Ziklag is where you rise.

Because after Ziklag comes recovery.
After recovery comes promotion.
After promotion comes influence.

Ziklag is the sound of the Archer pulling back for the final time before release.

When you stand in your own Ziklag moments, you can declare with confidence:

My ashes are not my ending.
My loss is not the last word.
My God has not abandoned His aim.
My comeback is already in motion.
My promotion is closer than it appears.
My Ziklag is the birthplace of my next level.

Heaven knows exactly where you are.
Heaven knows exactly what was taken.
Heaven knows exactly how to recover it.

Ziklag is the proof that God finishes what He starts, and that every pullback carries a comeback inside it.

CHAPTER 14

THE LAUNCH: ROCKETS, ROWERS, WARRIORS, ARROWS

Before every launch, the world holds its breath. The atmosphere thickens. Pressure builds. Motion hides inside stillness. Forces assemble in silence before bursting into sound. That threshold moment, between immobility and acceleration, mirrors the spiritual season the church is stepping into. Heaven has been preparing a launch far greater than any individual breakthrough. It is a collective propulsion of sons, daughters, communities, and nations into Kingdom purpose. Everything up to this point, pullback, wind-up, hush, alignment, refinement, has been leading to this singular command: *launch.*

There is a rising momentum: believers sensing pushback just before being fired forward, global shaking announcing Heaven's readiness, churches entering seasons of divine expansion, and nations trembling under the weight of what God is about to reveal. The imagery comes together here, at the moment of lift-off.

This chapter explores four prophetic metaphors—rowers, rockets, warriors and arrows—each revealing an aspect of Heaven's launch dynamics.

Launch is not simply movement. Launch is the moment Heaven says, *"Go now."*
Launch is when the tension becomes thrust.
Launch is when the arrow leaves the Archer's hand, the rocket leaves its pad, the rower drives backward to surge forward, and the warrior steps onto the battlefield with courage shaped in hidden places.

PROPHETIC MOTION IN REVERSE

There is something profoundly prophetic about rowing. At first glance, the movement seems illogical; rowers sit facing backward, pulling in the opposite direction of their destination. Their eyes do not rest on where they are going; they rest on the one leading the boat. Their strength does not emerge from pushing forward; it emerges from pulling back!

I want to highlight this symbol: *"like rowers going backward is the way to move forward."*
Rowing is the Kingdom's reminder that divine movement rarely mirrors natural logic. God often asks His people to pull back so He can thrust them forward. He often positions them to look at Him rather than at their destination. He trains them to follow His voice, His rhythm, His direction, rather than relying on their own visual clarity.

Rowers reveal three truths about launch:
1. Forward motion requires backward posture
The greatest strides in the Kingdom often happen when you surrender, retreat into the secret place, or allow God to reposition

your life. The world views backward motion as loss; Heaven views it as momentum.

2. Direction belongs to the Leader, not the rower
Rowers trust the one guiding the boat. They do not look where they are going, they trust the instructions given. This mirrors the life of faith, where clarity often comes after motion begins.

3. Timing is everything
Rowers move in unity with the call of their leader. When the timing is off, power is wasted. When timing aligns, movement becomes effortless. Launch seasons require that same unity with God's rhythm.

The church has been rowing through a season of what felt like retreat: pressing backward, digging deep, facing unexpected storms. Yet all this backward motion has been generating power. Now the Spirit is signaling stroke forward. The launch is here!

THE EARTH RESISTS WHAT HEAVEN RELEASES

There is a reason rocket scientists speak of "max Q," the moment of greatest atmospheric pressure. During launch, a rocket trembles, rattles and shakes as unimaginable forces collide: gravity resisting lift, pressure pushing against thrust, and the earth refusing to release what Heaven is elevating.

Breakthrough often comes with shaking, and that global instability signals not collapse, but launch. Just as rockets shake most violently at the moment of ascent, believers and churches often feel the strongest resistance right before lift-off.

Rockets teach us four prophetic laws of launch:
1. Shaking is confirmation

The shaking proves you are moving. The pressure proves you are rising. The resistance proves the assignment is real. When everything trembles, Heaven is burning away what cannot ascend with you.

2. Lift-off begins before motion is visible

A rocket's engines ignite long before it leaves the pad. The fire, thrust and pressure build internally before a single inch of movement becomes visible. Likewise, believers often experience inward fire, divine restlessness, spiritual pressure and prophetic stirring before their breakthrough becomes public.

3. The atmosphere changes as you ascend

Once a rocket breaks through the lower atmosphere, the turbulence disappears and motion becomes smooth. Many believers experience the same: once they break through initial resistance, momentum becomes peaceful and natural.

4. Nothing can hold back propulsion ordained by Heaven

Once thrust exceeds gravity, launch becomes inevitable. This law echoes a theme: when God says "launch!", no force in hell or earth can restrain the release. Acceleration sweeps aside opposition.

Rocket imagery reminds us that intense shaking is the soil of breakthrough. The world may resist what Heaven is releasing, but Heaven never yields to resistance.

WARRIORS RELEASED FOR VICTORY

Many believers have walked through a season that felt like pure survival. You held on through pressure. You kept your faith steady in storms. You stood your ground while darkness pressed in. And yet something inside you sensed that survival could never be your permanent identity. God never designed His people to live in a defensive crouch. The church was born to advance.

Right now, the Lord is raising, aiming, and steadying many of His people like arrows pulled back against a bowstring for the triumph He has already prepared. That shift changes everything. Warriors carry themselves differently when they know how the story ends. Confidence rises. Courage sharpens. Their whole posture comes alive.

This launch marks the moment when survivors become warriors. It's the turning of the heart from reacting to the enemy to responding to God, from merely holding ground to stepping into new territory with conviction.

Warriors forged in this kind of season fight with a God-given clarity. Survivors wonder, *"Will I make it?"* Warriors breathe, *"I was made for this."* They carry a deep awareness of who they are, the authority they've been given, and the assignment God has placed in their hands. Their confidence doesn't come from the absence of conflict but from Heaven's settled outcome.

They also understand that many of the battles rising around them sit on ground connected to their inheritance. Giants don't gather randomly. They show up on land God intends to give His people. This is why warriors don't shrink back from confrontation. They step forward with discernment, knowing that obedience opens doors the enemy tried to close.

And true warriors aren't driven by adrenaline or emotion. Their movement is shaped by God's voice. They wait for His signal—"pursue", "advance", "cross over", "rise" - and when it comes, they move with precision that only comes from being trained in the quiet places.

This generation of believers has been shaped in pressure, refined in wilderness seasons, strengthened in long stretches of waiting. None of it weakened them. Every moment prepared them. Heaven is releasing warriors of victory.

Arrows have carried the heartbeat of this book because they carry the heartbeat of God's prophetic imagery. They speak of precision, purpose, and a path guided by the Archer Himself. When God releases an arrow, it never drifts aimlessly. It flies with purpose woven into its design.

Every part of preparation suddenly reveals its value the moment the arrow is sent. The sanding produces speed. The straightening gives stability. The balancing creates unwavering focus. The polishing shapes the aerodynamics that cut through resistance. What felt tedious becomes fuel for impact.

Launch teaches us that release is not the true beginning; it simply unveils what has been crafted out of sight. The arrow doesn't guide itself through the air - trust takes over, and faith becomes the trajectory. All the surrender that took place before release becomes motion after release.

The long pullback felt slow, even painful at times. But the moment the arrow flies, everything accelerates. This is why breakthrough rarely matches the timetable of waiting. Years of quiet work often lead to moments of sudden momentum.

And when the Archer aims, impact is certain. Heaven never wastes an arrow. When God sends you, He intends fruitfulness.

The global church stands on the edge of this moment. The waiting has done its work. The tension has steadied hearts. The quiet has sharpened focus. Now comes the release. And as God sends

His people forward, the world will witness the craftsmanship He invested in the hidden years.

Many churches around the world are in a Ziklag-to-launch transition, moving from refinement to rapid expansion, from hiddenness to harvest, from preparation to outpouring. The church is not stepping into decline; it is stepping into deployment.

This launch is not limited to numerical growth. It includes:

- Global evangelistic acceleration
- Prophetic clarity and boldness
- Miraculous outpourings that draw the hungry
- A surge of prodigals returning home
- New wineskins stretching to hold new wine
- A shift from maintenance to movement

Churches that endured pressure, pruning, loss or restructuring are discovering that Heaven has been aiming them for something much larger than previous seasons could hold. Many will experience sudden doors opening in nations, sudden harvest outpourings, sudden financial miracles for Kingdom projects, sudden influence in their regions, and sudden waves of new disciples hungry for truth.

Old wineskins will burst—they cannot contain the scale of outpouring Heaven is releasing. The launch requires capacity that only the pullback season could create.

SUPERNATURAL HARVEST DEMANDS SUPERNATURAL LAUNCH

The size of the coming harvest demands a launch greater than human strategy. It will require supernatural timing, supernatural unity, supernatural boldness, and supernatural empowerment by the Spirit. What is coming is a force that will reshape regions.

Harvest requires launch because harvest requires workers who are not entangled, distracted or immobilized. It requires believers who are ready to fly the moment the Archer releases them.

This harvest will not be confined to church buildings. It will appear in businesses, schools, government spaces, entertainment industries, digital arenas, and unexpected nations. The Spirit is releasing arrows into fields that have never been touched by the gospel. The church is being launched not into comfort zones but into mission fields.

Heaven's launch is always tied to humanity's salvation.

PART V: THE MARK OF HOPE

HOPE: THE ULTIMATE COMEBACK

Hope stands as one of the most powerful forces in the Kingdom. It is not soft optimism or sentimental comfort; hope is spiritual propulsion. It moves the soul toward its destination even when circumstances appear motionless. Hope is the steady companion in the pullback, the quiet fire in the hush, the inner strength in the stretch, and the spark that erupts the moment breakthrough arrives. If faith is the engine, hope is the fuel. Hope takes everything God has spoken and pulls the future into the present, anchoring you in what has not yet manifested but already belongs to you.

Throughout Scripture and across every story of human redemption, hope is always the beginning of resurrection. Hope announces that the end you feared is not the end God wrote. Hope says your Ziklag is not your burial plot but your beginning. Hope whispers truth into ashes. Hope looks at empty ground and sees harvest. Hope sees what your natural eyes cannot. This theme echoes often, God turning setbacks into setups, seeds buried only to bloom, and the constant Kingdom principle that when things appear silent, Heaven is preparing something extraordinary. Hope stands at the center of that truth, interpreting divine intention when everything else feels uncertain.

Hope carries motion within it. It pushes the heart toward God's promises long before breakthrough becomes visible. Spiritual propulsion often begins the moment you choose to believe that what God said carries more authority than what your circumstances show. Hope activates movement when your life looks still, progression when your season feels paused, and courage when fear tries to immobilize you.

Hope does not wait for perfect conditions. Hope creates forward motion in imperfect conditions. The rower moving backward before surging forward mirrors this principle. The motion seems counterintuitive, and yet it places the boat in the correct position for acceleration. Hope operates the same way. It moves contrary to the world's expectation. When everything pulls backward, hope harnesses that pull as momentum. When life feels like it's in reverse, hope becomes the thrust that promises forward motion.

Believers often sense pressure and tension right before release. Hope is the force interpreting that tension correctly. Hope does not see the pullback as loss; it sees propulsion forming behind the scenes. Hope senses launch coming even when the natural world sees nothing but strain. Hope becomes the inner cry saying, *"This will not end in defeat. Something is being prepared."*

Propelled by hope, the spirit stretches further than fear allows. It reaches beyond discouragement. It holds the line when nothing moves. It waits with expectation rather than resignation. Hope strengthens the hands of those who feel weak and steadies the gaze of those who feel overwhelmed. Hope is not passive. Hope is powerful. Hope is movement waiting for manifestation.

HOPE RISING WHERE LOSS ONCE RULED

Hope does its greatest work in places that feel barren. Hope stands in the exact same soil where disappointment grows and declares that new life can still emerge. It takes territory back from sorrow. It redeems emotional landscapes devastated by unexpected storms. It refuses to allow loss to become identity. Instead, hope transforms loss into a launching platform for resurrection.

Ziklag illustrates this beautifully. Loss consumed David for a moment: family gone, possessions stolen, home destroyed. But hope resurfaced when he strengthened himself in the Lord. That turning, where sorrow surrendered to divine courage, marks the rebirth of destiny. Hope stepped into the ashes and refused to let despair define the outcome. It spoke louder than grief. It insisted on recovery even before instruction came. Hope set the stage for restoration long before David saw evidence that recovery was possible.

Many churches, leaders and believers are living in their own Ziklag moments, experiencing pressure, pruning, transition or unexpected loss, yet Heaven is preparing a resurrection that far outweighs the devastation. Hope rises in those environments because hope recognizes that what looks like the end is often the necessary clearing for something new.

Hope grows best in the cracks of broken seasons. It rises through disappointment, resists resignation, and builds courage where defeat tried to settle. Hope rebuilds what grief dismantled. It restores confidence where fear once lived. It reclaims vision where confusion tried to suffocate calling.

When hope rises where loss once ruled, destiny begins to breathe again.

Hope restores direction. When hope awakens, vision sharpens. Purpose reappears. Targets come back into focus. The soul begins to see not only where it is, but where it is being aimed.

During the pullback, the arrow cannot see its target. All it feels is pressure. All it senses is the stretch. But once the Archer aligns it, hope recognizes the aim. Hope steadies what fear once rattled. Hope becomes the internal compass pointing toward the promises of God.

This is why hope restores passion. Passion flows where vision lives. When hope revives the awareness that God is still aiming your life with intention, passion reignites. Worship deepens. Obedience strengthens. Prayer becomes bold rather than timid. Hope infuses spiritual stamina and awakens dormant expectation. It brings clarity to purpose and reveals assignment with fresh intensity.

Hope restores courage because courage cannot exist without expectation of good. Fear thrives when the future looks dark. Courage rises when light emerges. Hope is that light. It shines onto uncertain paths and reveals that God has not abandoned His work. It assures the heart that the journey still holds promise. Hope does not erase hardship but transforms how you face hardship.

Many have been focused on storms, winds and waves rather than on Jesus, the Author and Finisher of their faith. Hope redirects that gaze. It turns eyes away from the storm and fixes them on the One who speaks peace over turbulent waters. Hope restores the aim when distractions blurred it. Hope brings the heart back into alignment with the upward call.

HOPE AS THE FRUIT OF SURRENDER, TRUST, TENSION AND BREAKTHROUGH

Hope grows slowly, seeded in surrender, watered in trust, shaped in tension and strengthened in breakthrough.

It is not born overnight. It forms within seasons when the soul must lean deeper into God's character rather than into visible outcomes.

Hope is the fruit of surrender
When you surrender the desire to control timelines, manipulate outcomes or rush God's process, hope blooms. Surrender creates space for expectation, because you finally allow God to lead the story. The arrows shaped by the Archer are sanded, straightened, balanced, polished. That shaping requires surrender. Hope emerges when the arrow stops resisting the Archer's hand.

Hope is the fruit of trust
Trust is the decision to believe God's nature over your circumstances. Trust is not blind; it is rooted in the faithfulness of God seen throughout Scripture and history. Trust allows hope to rise even when the path feels hidden. Trust knows that God finishes what He starts and that every promise carries His reputation. Hope grows in that soil.

Hope is the fruit of tension
Tension is uncomfortable, but it deepens reliance on God. The stretching, the silence, the waiting, the holy hush, these mo-

ments purify motives and refine desires. Hope matures in tension because it learns to anchor itself in eternity rather than in temporary comfort.

Hope is the fruit of breakthrough

When breakthrough arrives, hope expands. It remembers the faithfulness of God in the hardest moments and strengthens confidence for future battles. Breakthrough reinforces hope for everything ahead.

Hope is both process and result. It is both journey and destination. It is formed in adversity and displayed in victory. Hope reveals God's presence not only in the relief of breakthrough but in the shaping that preceded it.

BELIEVERS ARE NOT STUCK; THEY ARE IN A DIVINE SETUP.

This is hope's final declaration. It reframes the entire narrative. It takes seasons of delay and assigns purpose to them. It takes moments of confusion and infuses them with destiny. It takes stillness and redefines it as preparation. It takes hardship and reveals it as training.

Hope speaks into the pullback and states, "God is aiming you."
Hope speaks into the hush and says, "He is focusing you."
Hope speaks into the waiting and whispers, "He is preparing you."
Hope speaks into pressure and reminds you, "He is strengthening you."
Hope speaks into launch and celebrates, "You were made for this moment."

Hope is the lens that reveals the supernatural orchestration behind the scenes. It allows you to see your life not as random moments of suffering and blessing, but as carefully timed movements of an Archer who never wastes tension. Hope reveals that every difficulty is woven into a divine strategy to position you for impact.

When hope becomes the dominant truth in your spirit, fear loses its influence. Doubt loses its grip. Weariness loses its power. Hope gives you language for a future that the enemy tried to convince you would never arrive.

Hope is prophetic.

It sees beyond the surface.
It interprets silence as strategy.
It recognizes the Archer's fingerprints on every season.
It anticipates release with expectation rather than dread.

Hope transforms the believer into someone who lives from divine setup rather than human limitation.

Hope is God's signature written across your journey. It confirms that your life is not abandoned, forgotten or overlooked. It certifies that every season—wilderness, tension, waiting, loss, breakthrough—was designed with intention. Hope proves that God is not finished. Hope reveals that you are still in motion. Hope announces to every opposing force: *"This life belongs to Heaven."*

When hope marks your heart, you begin to:

- pray differently
- dream differently
- speak differently
- lead differently
- pursue differently
- recover differently
- occupy differently

Hope births boldness. It inflames desire. It restores resilience. It gives depth to worship and courage to obedience. It allows you to hold the bowstring of destiny without collapsing under pressure.

Hope is the spirit's reminder that the Archer has never lost sight of the target.
Hope is the steady truth that the pullback was necessary.
Hope is the breath before the launch, the strength in the release, the clarity in the aim, and the certainty of the comeback.

Your story does not end in defeat.
Your story ends in glory.
Your comeback is already in motion.

And hope is the banner waving over every chapter of your life declaring, "You are not stuck. You are in a divine setup."

CONCLUSION: AIMED & READY

There comes a moment at the end of every journey when the shaping is complete, the sanding has smoothed the rough edges, the stretching has settled into alignment, and the pullback has reached its full measure. It is the moment when the Archer lifts His gaze toward the horizon, feels the weight of the assignment in His hand, and prepares the arrow for release. This book has walked through the hidden work, the tension, the hush, the shaping, the surrender, the reset and the rise. Now the invitation stands clear and unmistakable: **you are aimed and ready.**

Heaven is not passive in this hour. Heaven is commissioning. A fresh wave of divine purpose is moving across the earth, calling believers into boldness, clarity and forward momentum. You were not formed in darkness only to remain unseen. You were not strengthened in pressure only to fall short of impact. You were not stretched so deeply only to stay grounded. Every shaping season has been leading to this moment when Heaven places you at full draw and whispers a final command:
"Be the arrow."

Being the arrow means yielding to the Archer's direction. It means allowing God to aim you at targets you never would have chosen, trusting His wisdom above your own desires. It means living with a posture ready for release, eyes fixed on Him, heart steady in waiting, spirit anchored in faith. It means embracing motion when He sends you, anointing your life for flight and impact only God can measure. Trusting the trajectory even if the path feels unfamiliar. Being the arrow is the ultimate act of surrender.

This commissioning is not soft. It is bold. It is the language of warriors, pioneers, reformers and prophets. It is the call to move in step with Heaven—to rise when commanded, retrieve what was stolen, occupy what belongs to you, and launch into the assignments the Spirit has prepared. It is an invitation into courage that refuses to shrink back, into confidence that refuses to waver, into obedience that refuses to stall, and into hope that refuses to die.

"I am certain that God, who began the good work within you, will continue his work until it is finally finished."
— Philippians 1:6

The Archer finishes what He starts. God never abandons the work of His hands. He completes the shaping. He perfects the alignment. He determines the timing. He protects the trajectory. He guards the flight. His promises are not abandoned midair; they fly until they hit their mark. This assurance is your inheritance. Everything He has spoken is still alive, still active, still pointed toward fulfillment. The target has not moved. His word has not expired. The call has not diminished.

Heaven's aim is relentless.

You may have walked through seasons that felt uncertain, times when tension made you question your readiness, when silence made you doubt your direction, when loss made you wonder if the promise was fading. Yet every moment has been part of a divine sequence. Pullback was never punishment. Waiting was never wasted. Pressure was never meaningless. Hiddenness was never abandonment. Every chapter of your life has been positioning you for impact greater than you imagined.

And now the Spirit announces that the days ahead will reveal the reason behind the tension. Breakthrough will confirm what hope already whispered. Momentum will reveal what faith carried in stillness. Acceleration will explain the waiting. Impact will justify the cost. You will look back and recognize that the Archer's hand was steady all along.

You were not reduced. You were refined.
You were not delayed. You were aligned.
You were not overlooked. You were prepared.
You were not stuck. You were in a divine setup.

This conclusion is not an ending, this is your commissioning moment. The bow is arched. The string is taut. The angle is set. Heaven has already calculated distance, speed, timing and impact. You stand positioned between the Archer's fingers and the horizon of your calling. Everything within you that once trembled is now strengthening. Everything that once hesitated is now awakening. The future is not resisting you, it is pulling you forward.

Now lift your heart, steady your breath, and step into the next chapter of your life with courage. The Archer's hand is faithful. His aim is perfect. His release is powerful. You were crafted for this moment. You are aimed and ready.

A PRAYER OF SURRENDER, ALIGNMENT, COURAGE AND FORWARD MOVEMENT

Father,
I surrender fully to Your hand. Shape me, steady me, align me
with Your purpose. Remove what cannot fly. Strengthen what
must endure. Straighten every place in me that leans away from
Your will. Prepare my heart to hold Your direction without fear.

Point me where You desire. Aim my life at the targets Heaven has chosen. Let my spirit rest in Your grip and let my mind quiet under Your voice. Teach me to trust Your angle, Your timing, Your trajectory and Your release. I yield every desire for control, every fear of missing the mark, and every doubt that rises in the waiting.

Anchor me in Your faithfulness.

Give me courage for forward movement. Fill me with boldness that stands firm, passion that burns steady, clarity that cuts through confusion and focus that endures every shaking. Position my feet in promise. Align my heart with destiny. Strengthen my faith to rise, retrieve and occupy everything You have prepared.

I declare that I am not stuck; I am in a divine setup.
You are finishing what You started.
Your promises are alive.
Your aim is perfect.
Your timing is sure.
Your plans will prevail.
Send me where You desire.
Release me when the moment comes.
Make my life an arrow in Your hand
—accurate, anointed, unstoppable.

In Jesus' name, Amen.

If this book has blessed you then consider getting the devotional workbook to help you establish all that God has revealed to you

BOOKS BY NICO SMIT

Nico Smit is an award-winning author with more than 8 published books, 4 of which are featured here.

He is a well-travelled, accomplished and respected international prophetic apostolic voice within the Christian community. With decades of experience in ministry Nico's mission is clear: to inspire and empower people to discover their God-given potential and live with unshakable faith. "Powerful Christian books for powerful people" is not just a motto for Nico, but a reflection of his desire to see his readers rise above their circumstances and live empowered by their faith. Nico's message transcends borders, cultures and denominations, resonating with anyone who is willing to step out in faith and believe in the power of miracles. Through his books, he shares not just theological insights but deeply personal stories of overcoming adversity. His works are inspired by his lived experiences, both the victories and the trials. Nico's approach to ministry and writing is based on personal experience, not theory. He writes his books from a place of firsthand knowledge of God's power in his own life and his encounters with others in their darkest hours. This authenticity is what makes his works stand out in a crowded market of Christian literature. His most recent books, including Miracles, Beyond The Crowd, Revival People, Gilgal to Bethel, and It's Time to Go Up!, are not just for intellectual growth, they are tools designed to change lives. Each book is a testament to the strength God makes available to anyone who comes to Him and aligns with divine purpose.

Alongside his published books, Nico has developed a range of devotional workbooks, prayer books, and Bible study guides designed to support individuals, groups, and churches in their Christian journeys.

Most of his books are now available as audio books.

He is lead pastor of RiverCity Church, based in Hobart, Tasmania, Australia and oversees its worldwide ministry network. Other functions include Chairman at Gateway Life Solutions LTD, Director at OCI Foundation LTD, pastor with Glory City Network, and a council member of the Australian Prophetic Council. He is a qualified clinical counselor. Born in Durban, South Africa, and married to Joe-Ann. They have two married children and five beautiful grandchildren.

www.ingramcontent.com/pod-product-compliance
Lightning Source LLC
LaVergne TN
LVHW051936070526
838200LV00078B/4959